Drawing has rules, the most important of which is to look carefully at
the shape that you want to draw, before you start drawing.
You can use several tools like:
Pencils, pens, colored pens, etc...
Then simplify drawing with geometric shapes, as in this book
And if you want to learn, you have to draw every day.

TOOLS

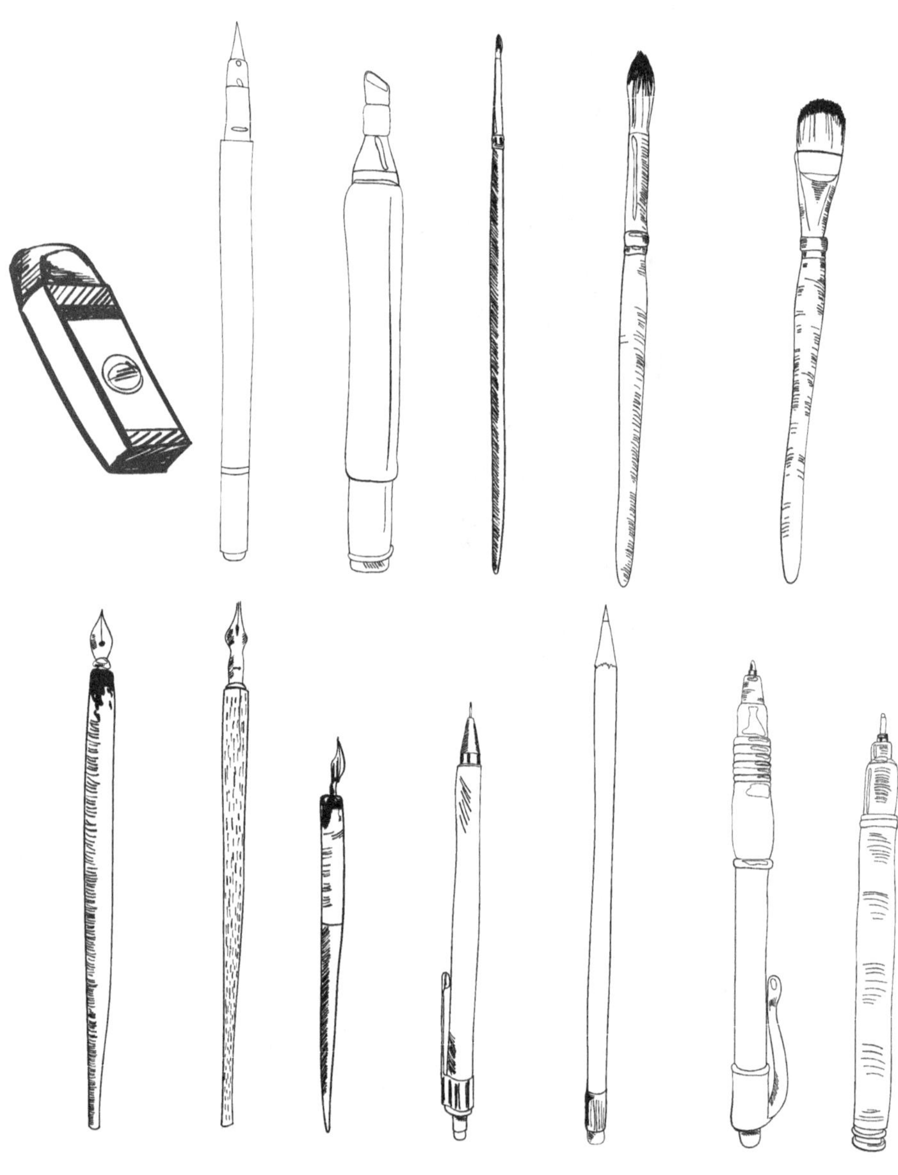

HOW TO DRAW

DRAWING TUTORIAL FOLWERS

| Look at the steps | Draw over the drawing | Repeat the drawing here |

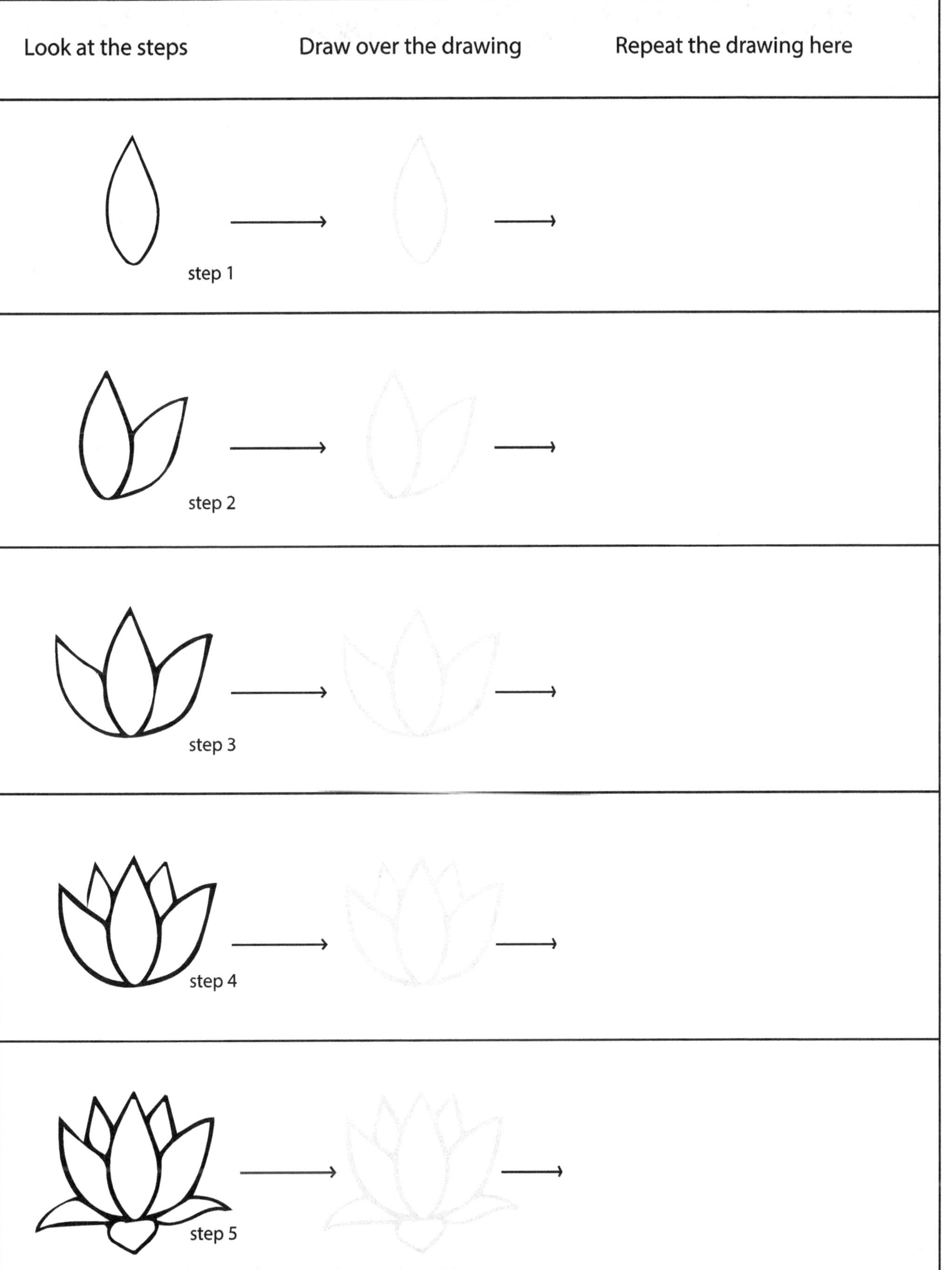

How to draw flowers

Step 1

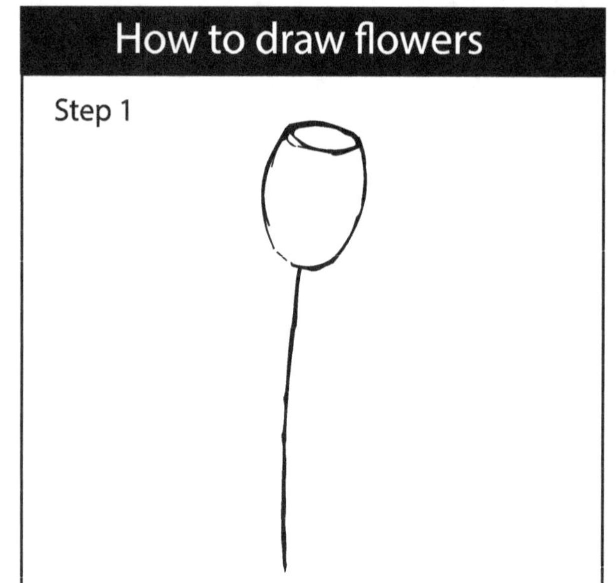

Step 1

Step 2

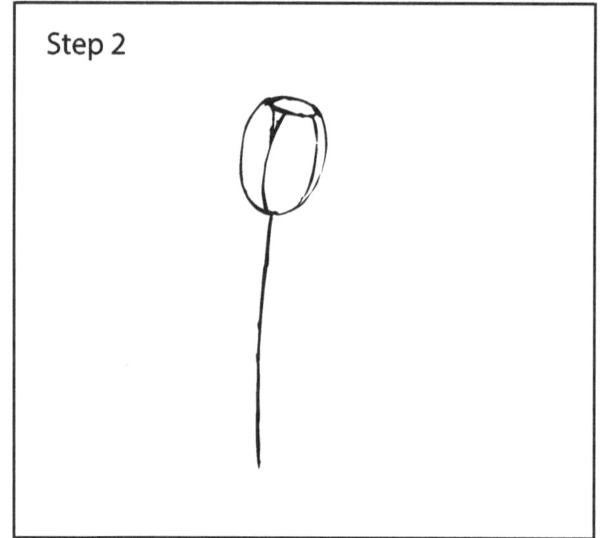

Step 2

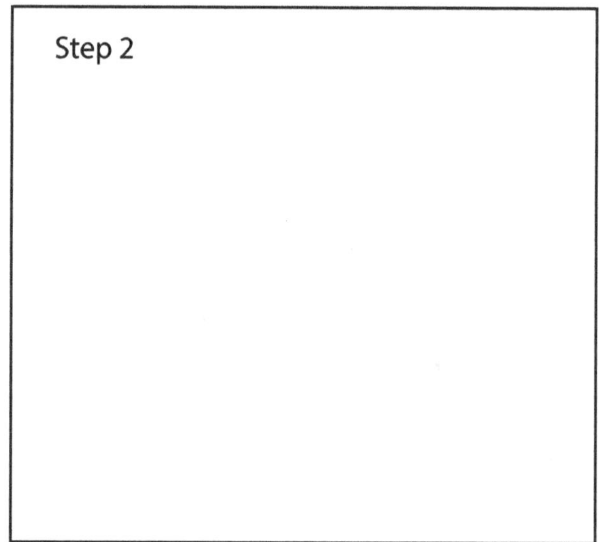

Step 3

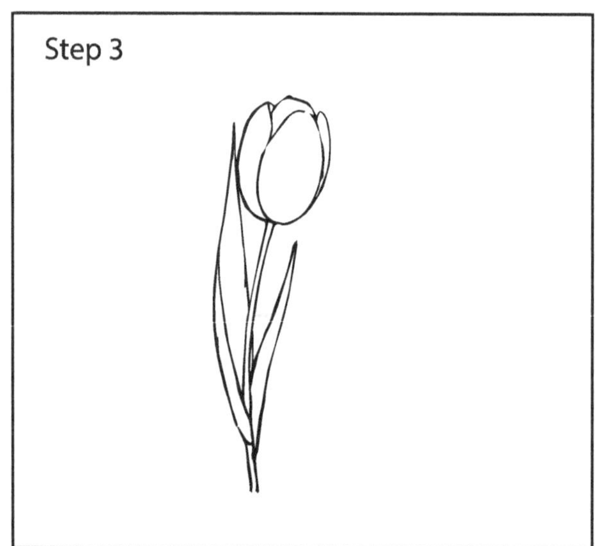

Step 3

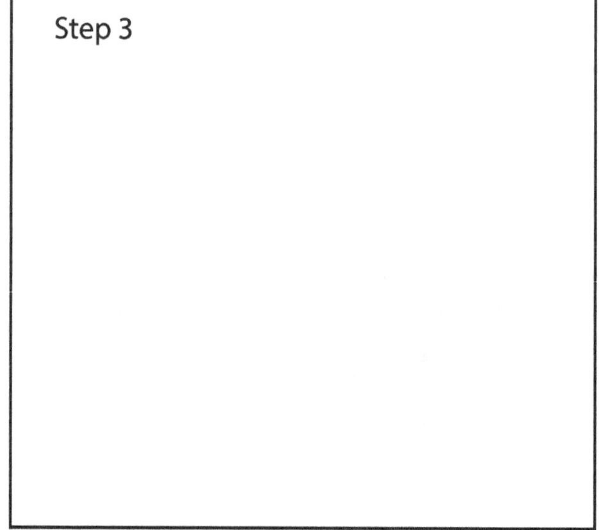

Step 1

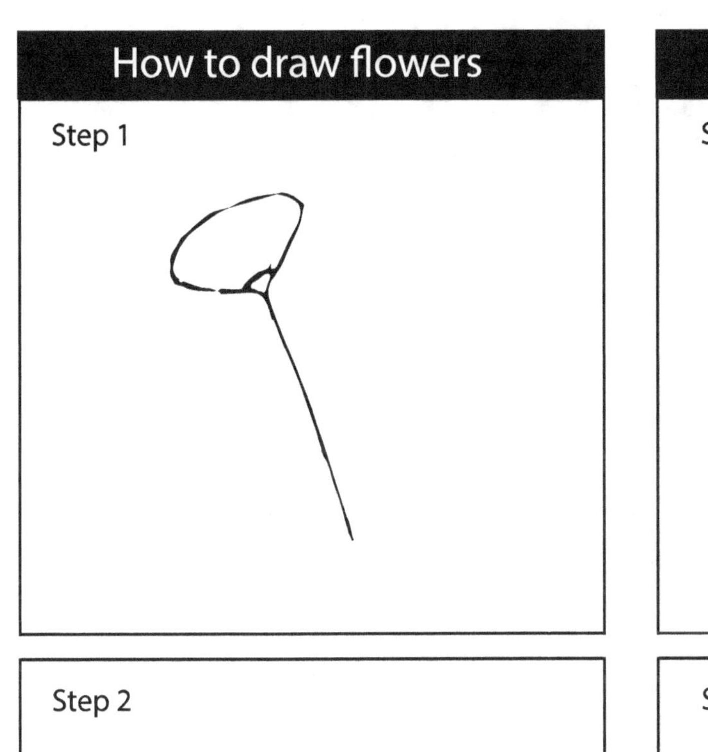

Step 1

Step 2

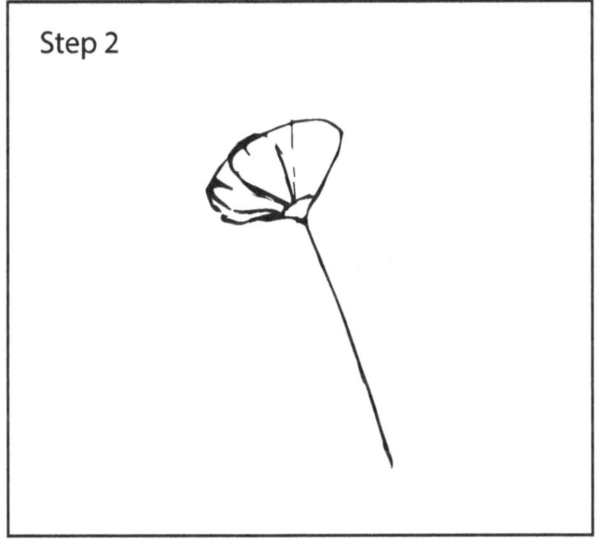

Step 2

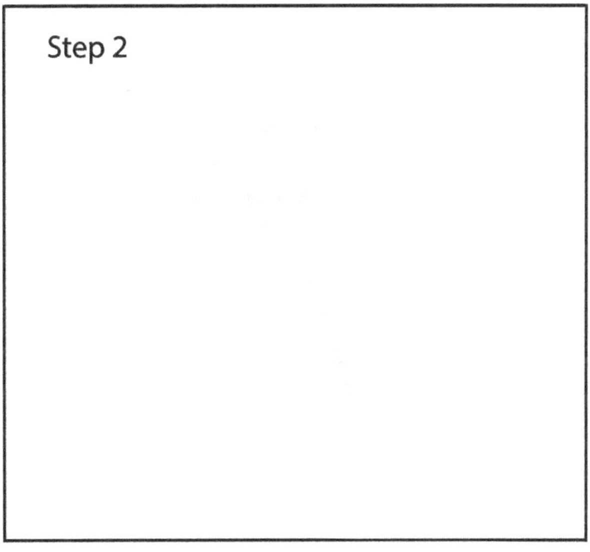

Step 3

Step 3

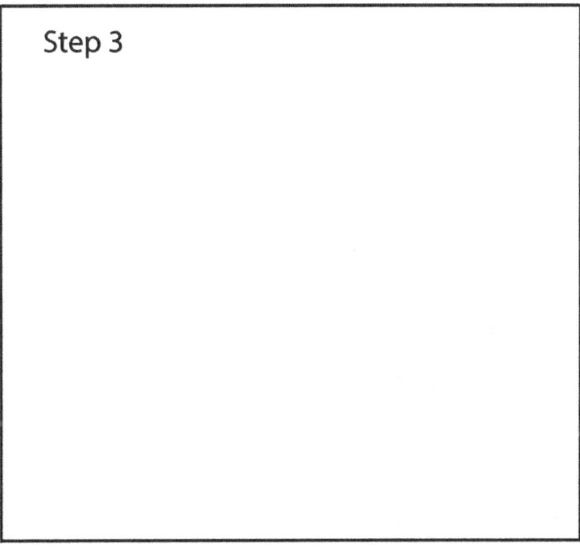

The Steps

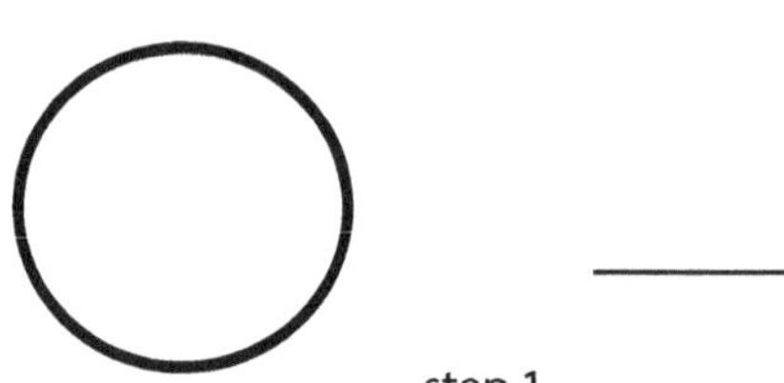

step 1

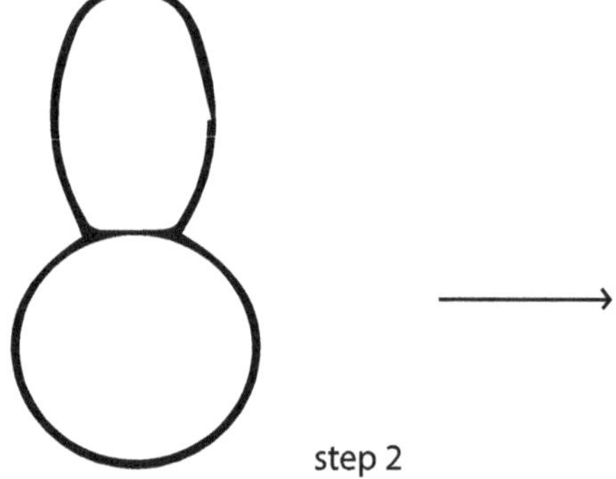

step 2

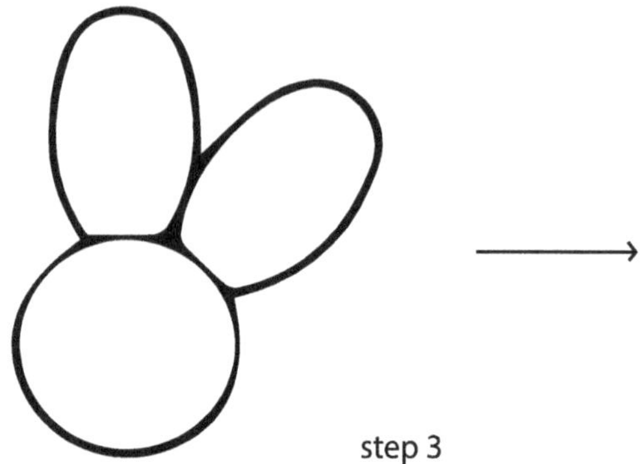

step 3

Draw the Following Steps

The Steps

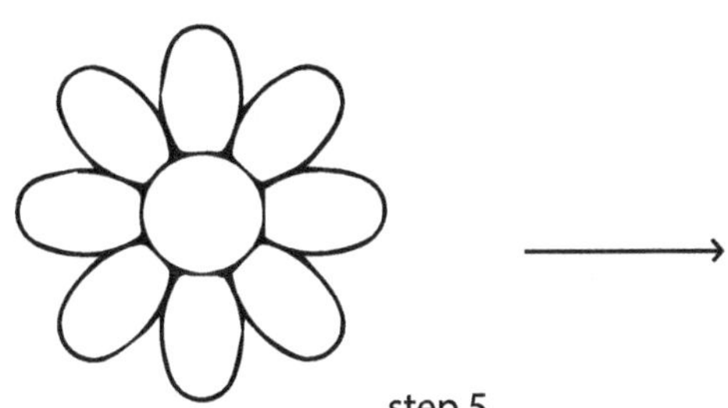

step 5

step 6

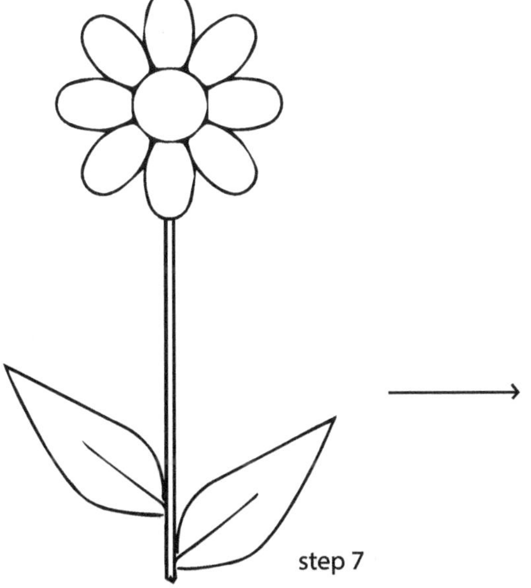

step 7

Draw the Following Steps

The Steps

Draw the Following Steps

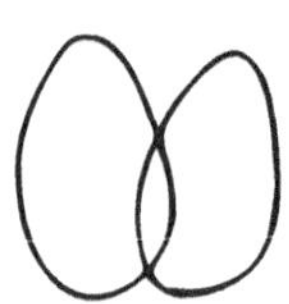

step 1

step 2

step 3

10

The Steps

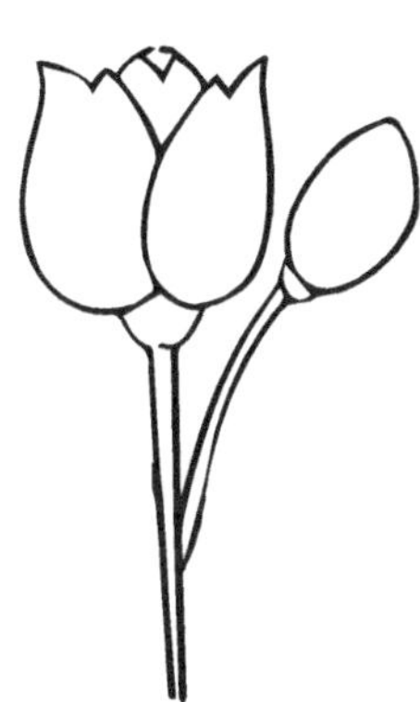

step 4

step 5

step 6

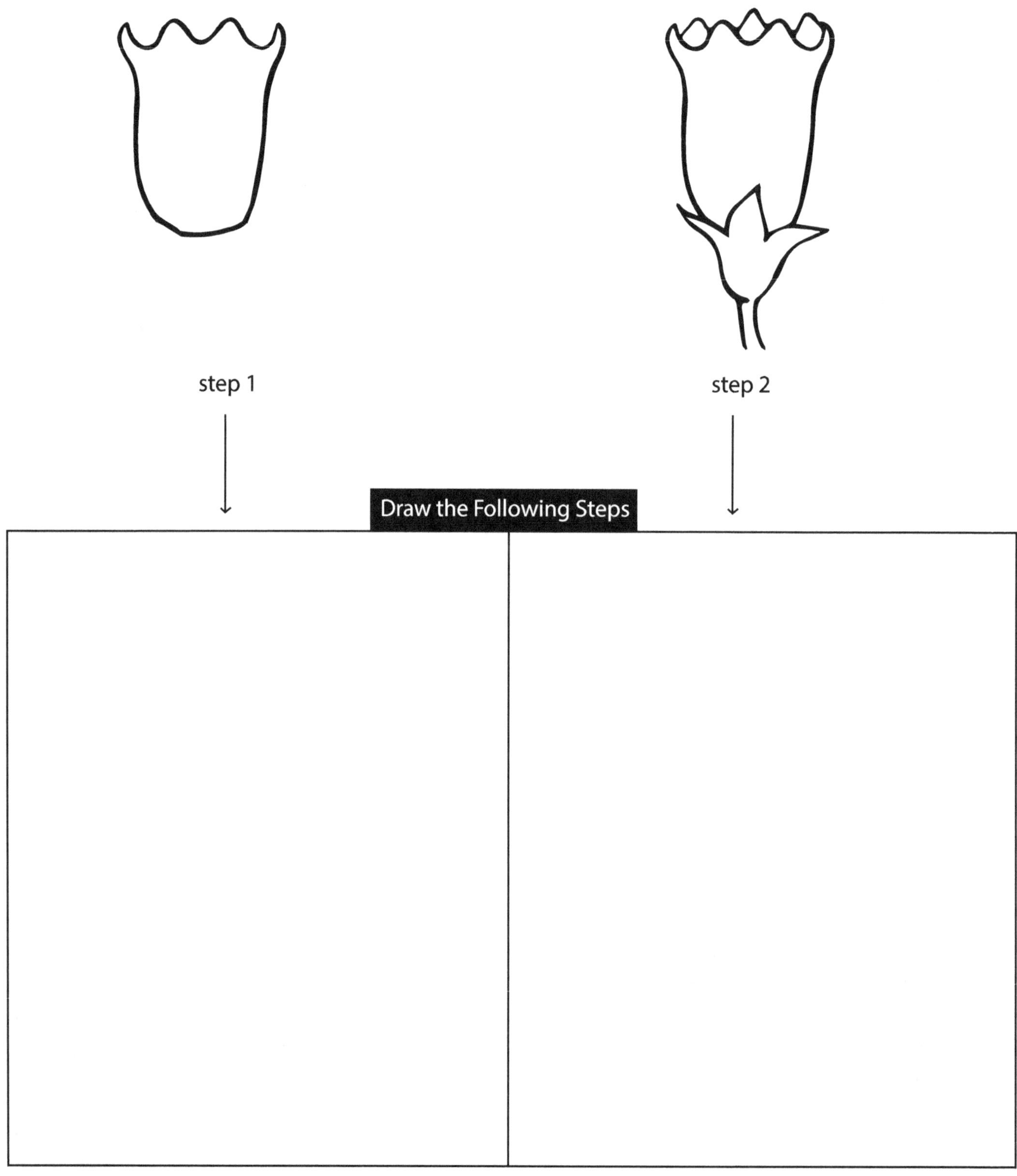

step 1
step 2
Draw the Following Steps

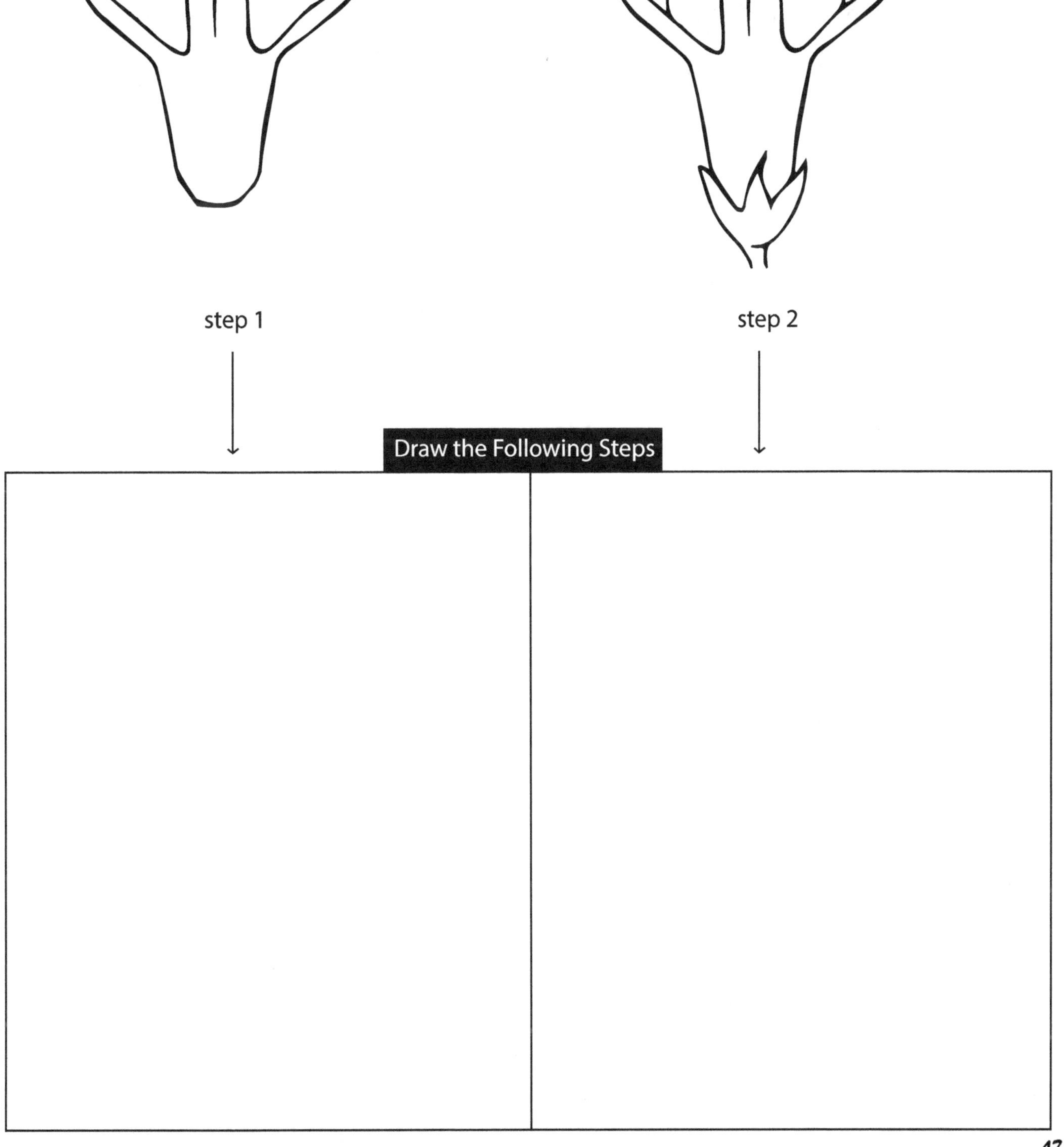

step 1
step 2
Draw the Following Steps

The Steps

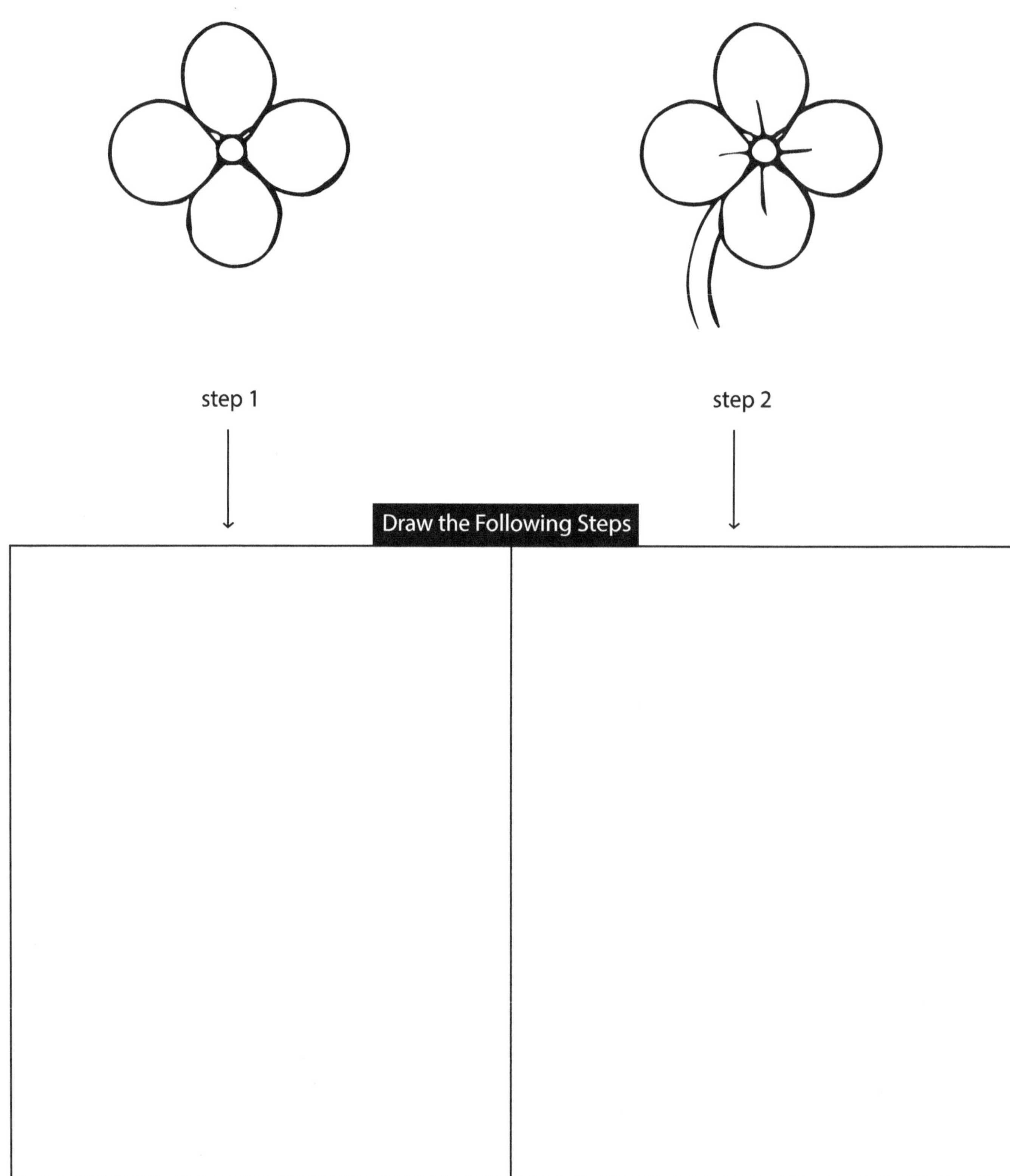

step 1

step 2

Draw the Following Steps

The Steps

Draw the Following Steps

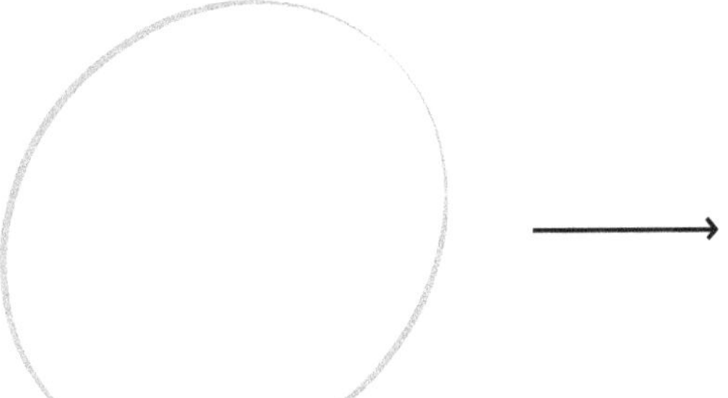

step 1

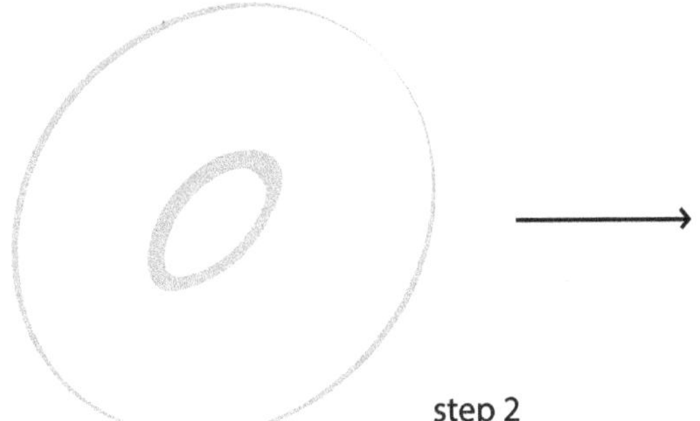

step 2

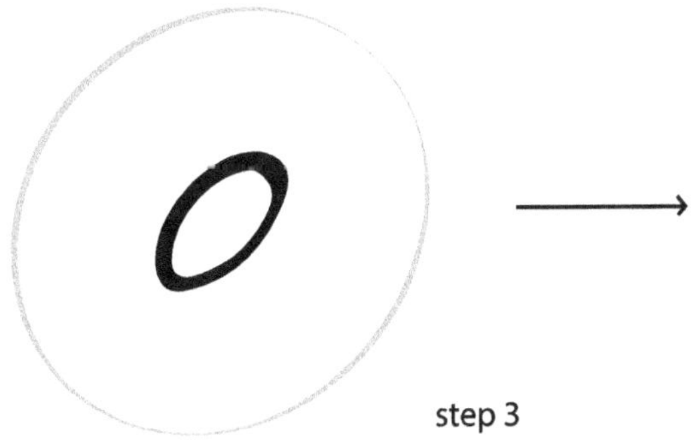

step 3

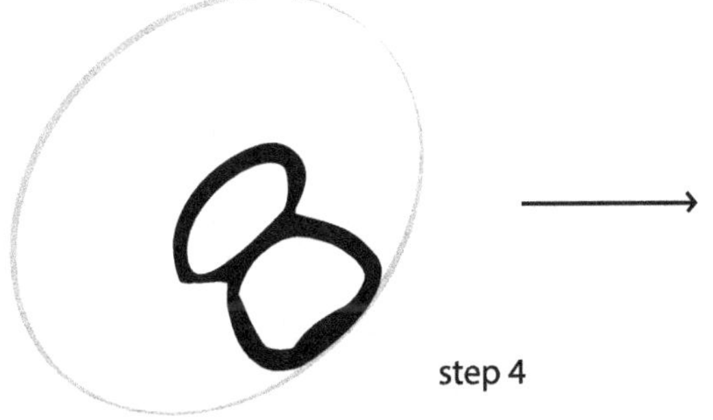

step 4

The Steps

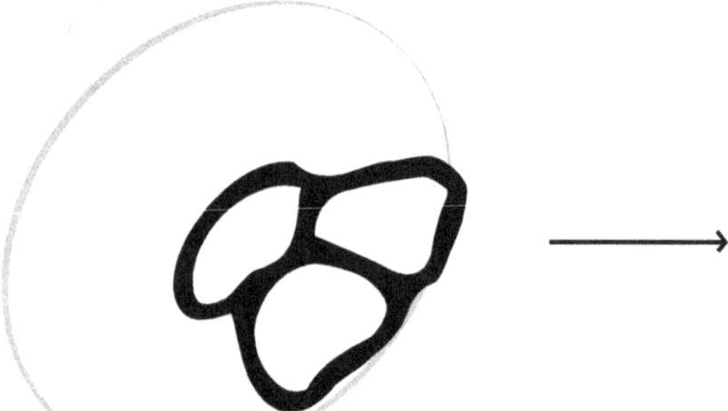

step 5

step 6

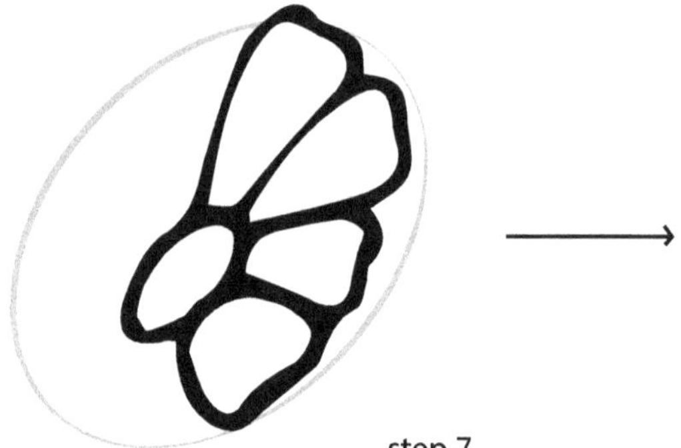

step 7

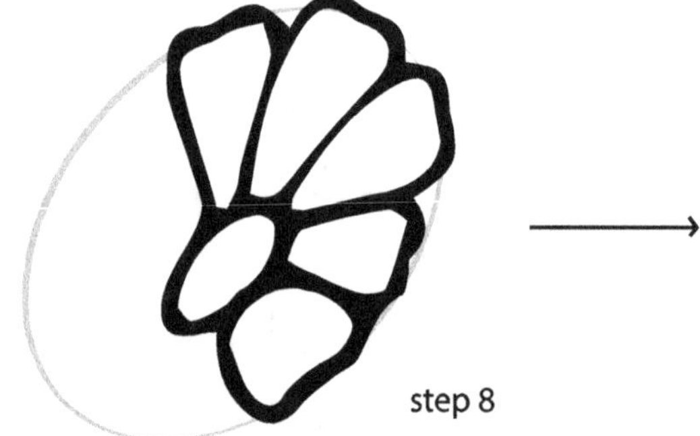

step 8

Draw the Following Steps

The Steps

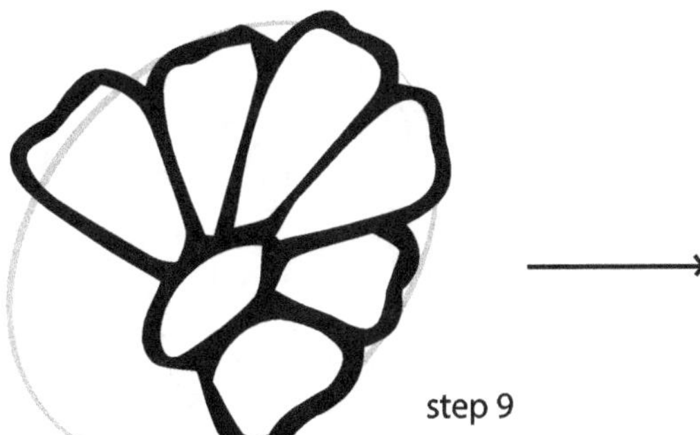

step 9

step 10

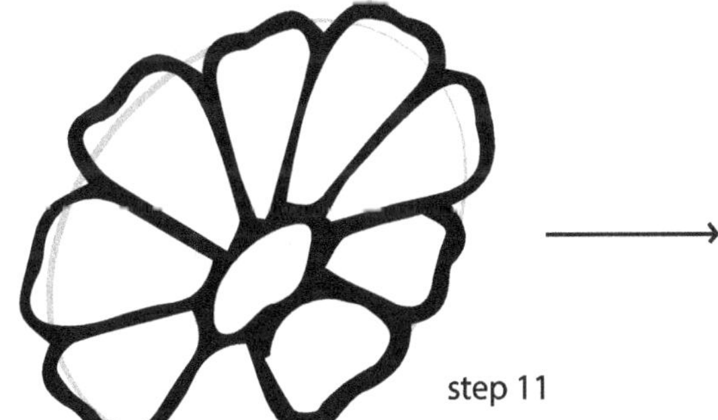

step 11

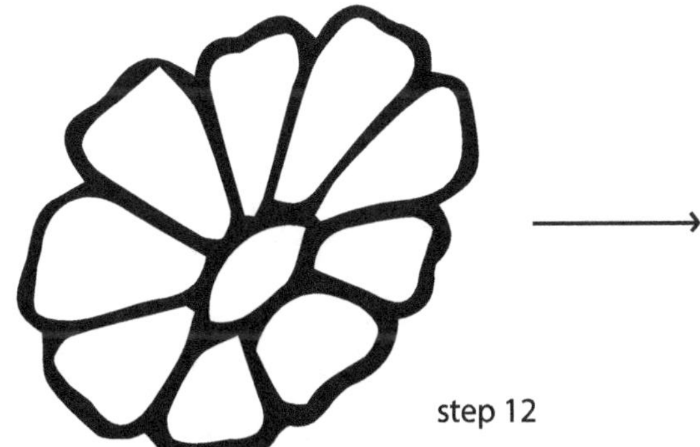

step 12

Draw the Following Steps

The Steps

Draw the Following Steps

step 13

step 14

step 15

step 16

DRAWING TUTORIAL MOTH

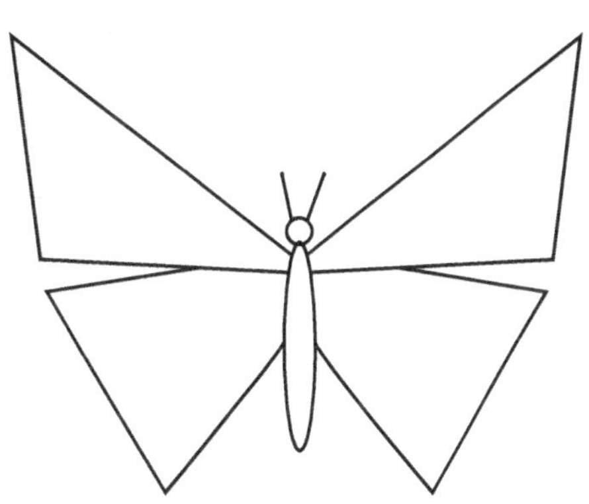

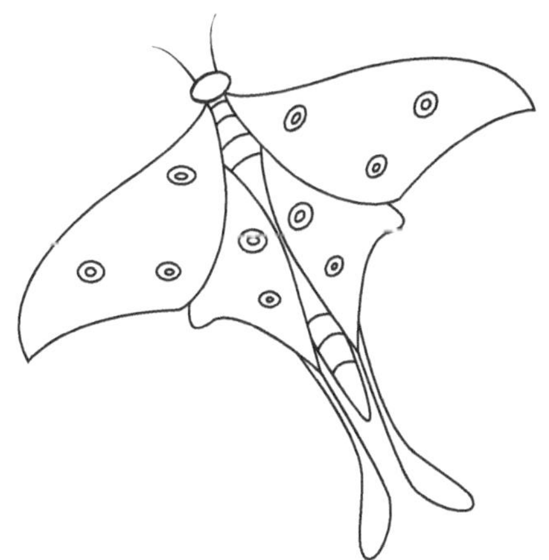

The Steps

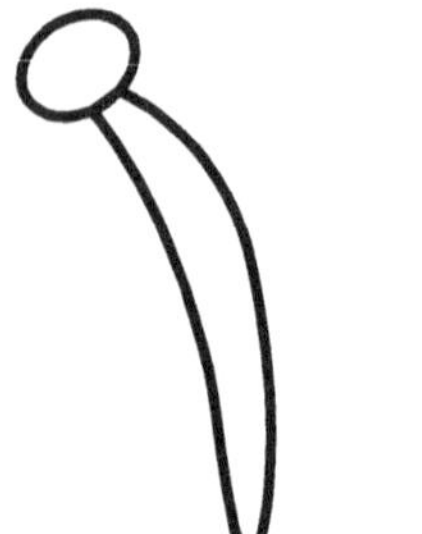

step 1

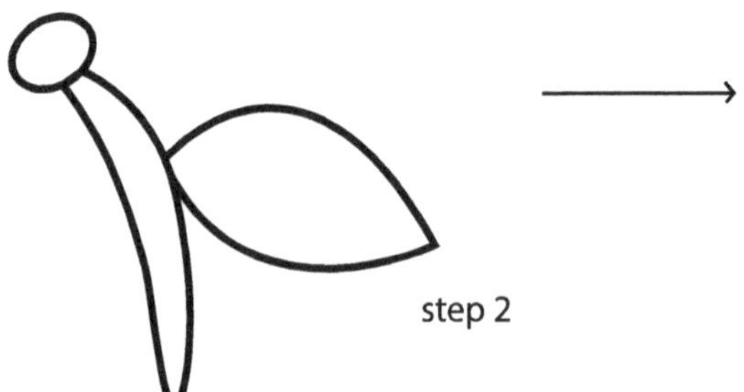

step 2

step 3

The Steps

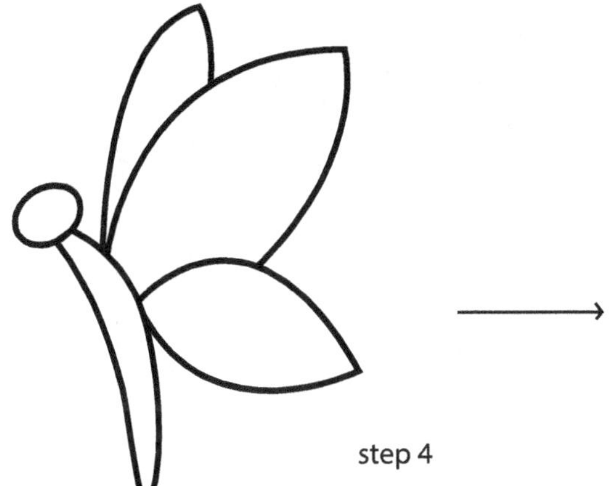

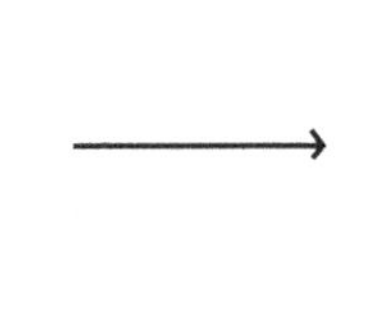

step 4

step 5

step 6

Draw the Following Steps

The Steps

Draw the Following Steps

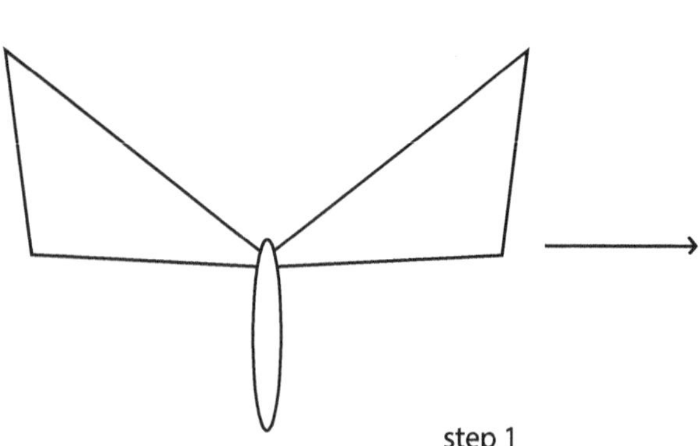

step 1

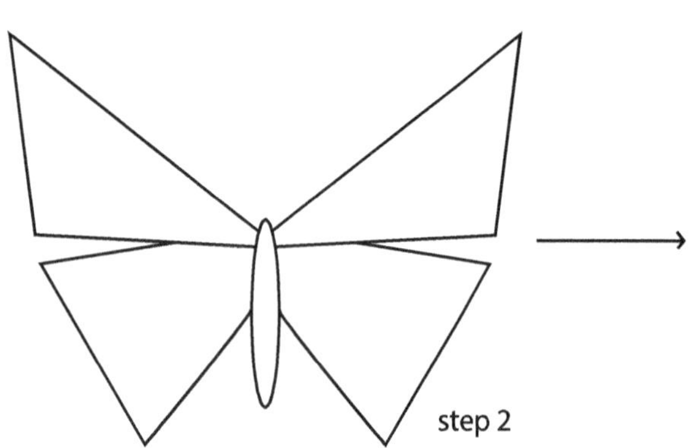

step 2

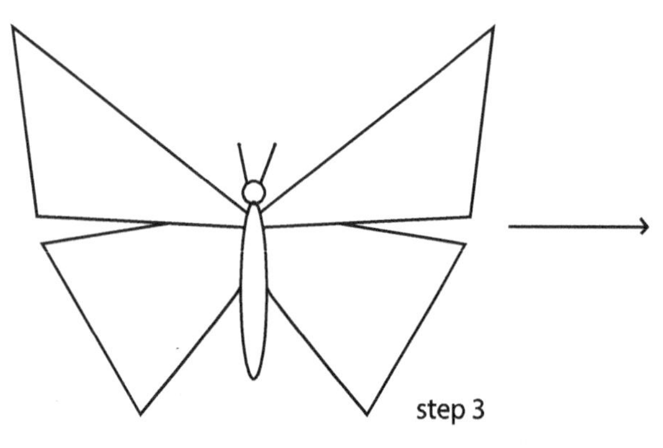

step 3

The Steps

Draw the Following Steps

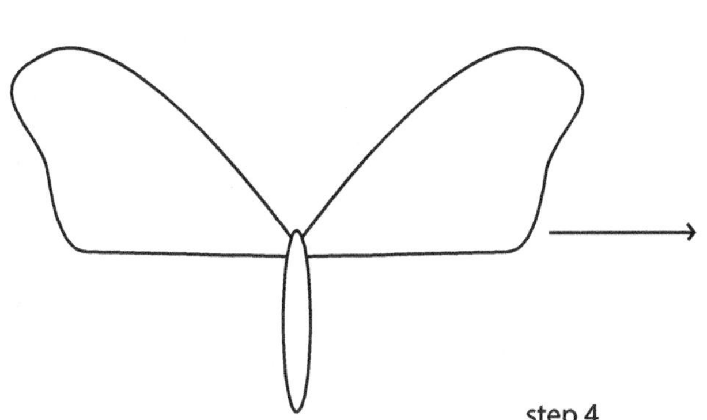

step 4

step 5

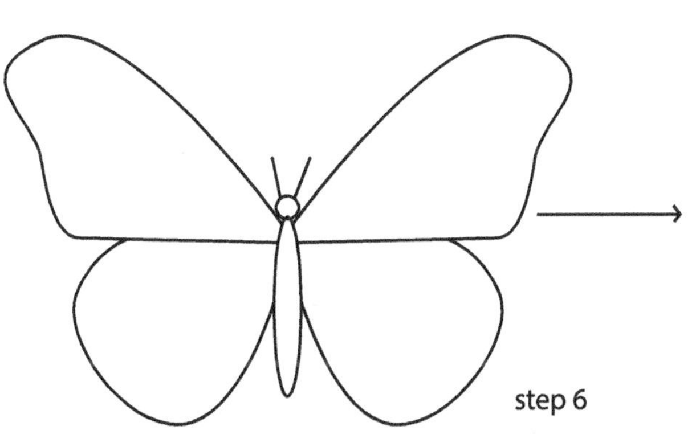

step 6

23

The Steps

Draw the Following Steps

step 1

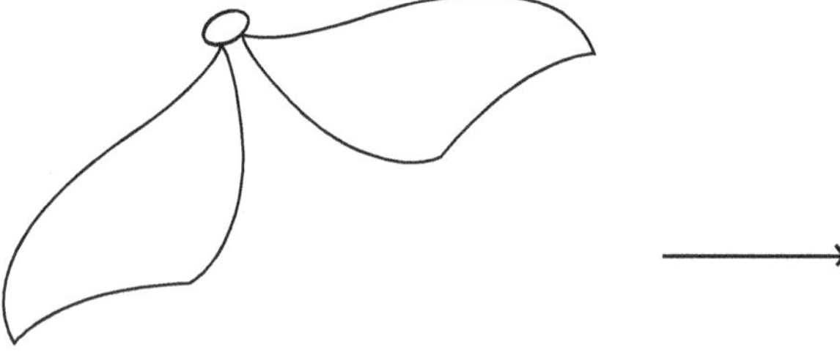

step 2

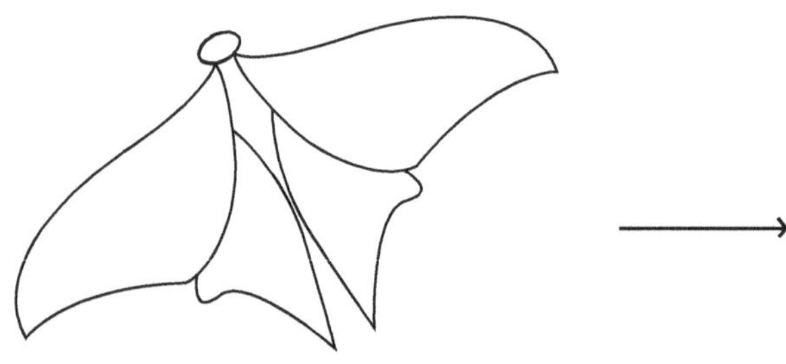

step 3

The Steps

Draw the Following Steps

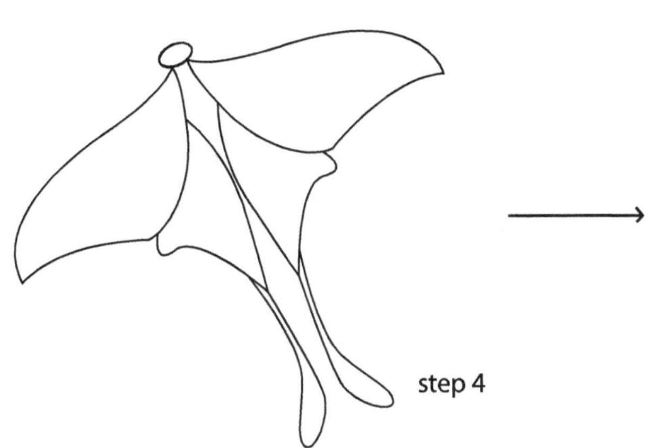
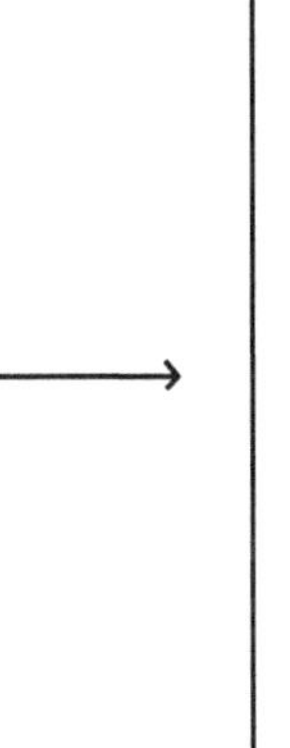

step 4

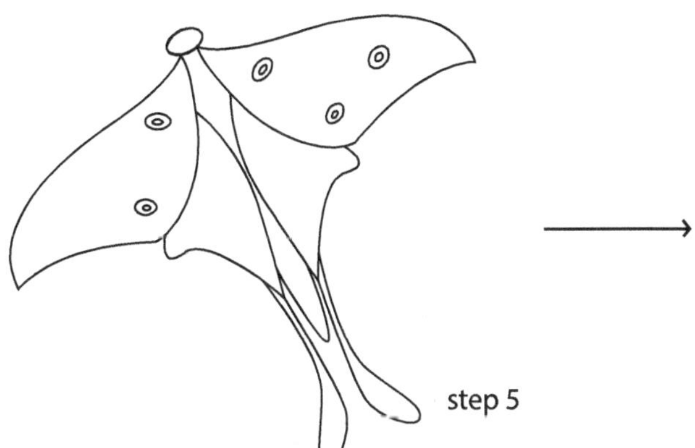

step 5

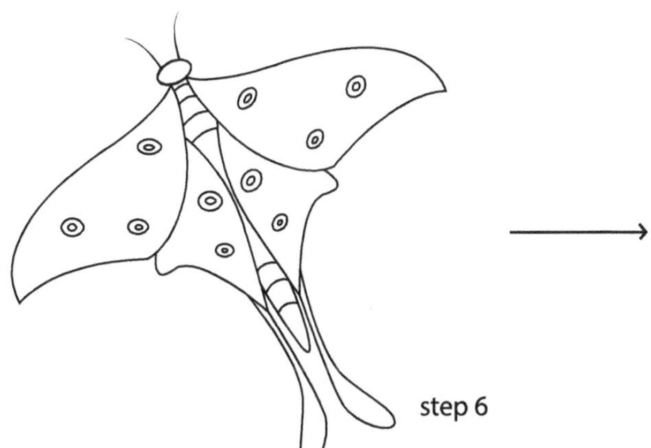

step 6

DRAWING TUTORIAL CATS

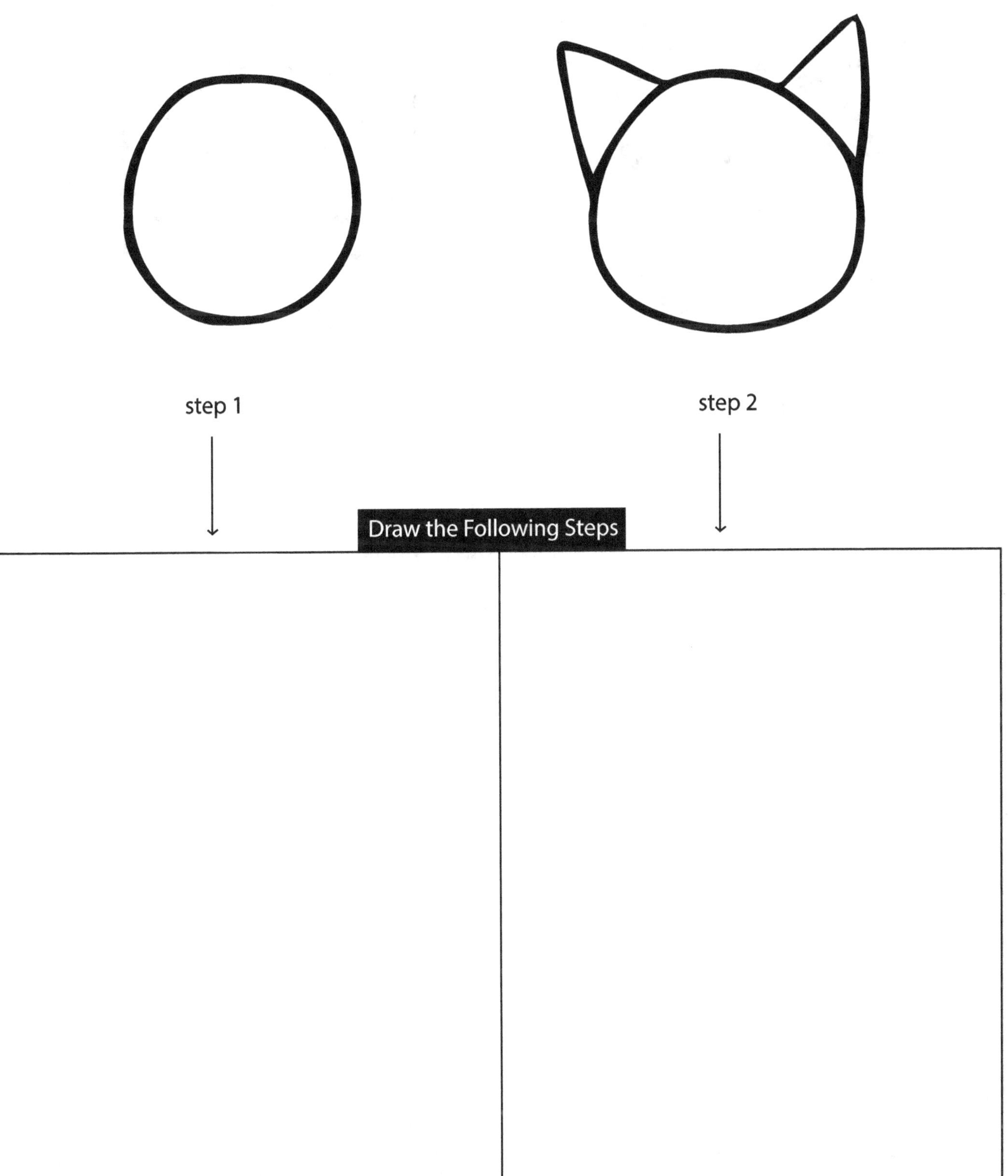
step 1
step 2
Draw the Following Steps

step 3

step 4

Draw the Following Steps

The Steps

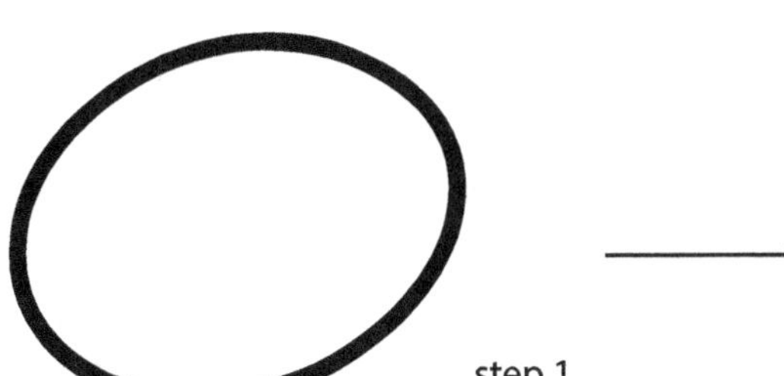

step 1

step 2

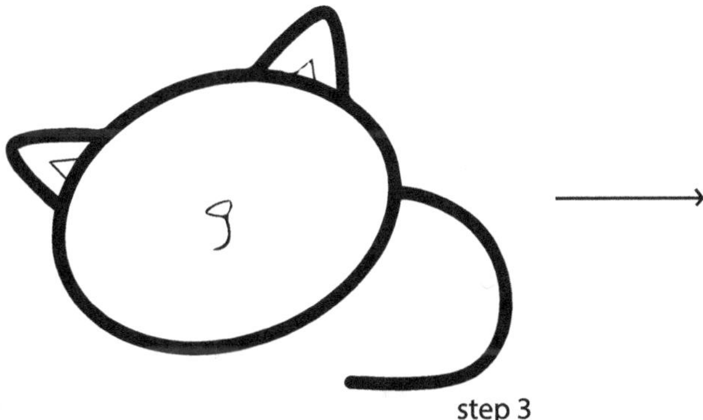

step 3

Draw the Following Steps

The Steps

step 4

step 5

step 5

Draw the Following Steps

The Steps

Draw the Following Steps

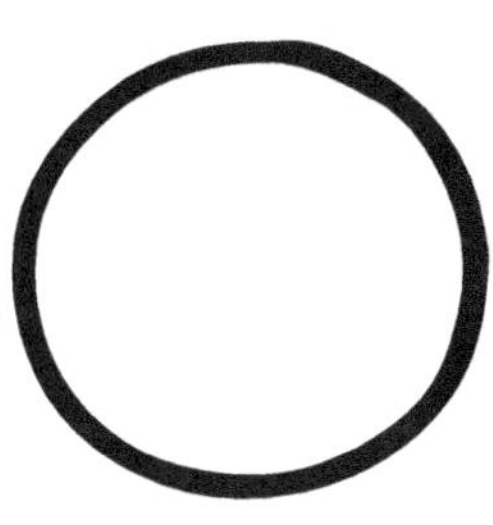

step 1

step 2

step 3

The Steps

Draw the Following Steps

step 4

step 5

step 6

The Steps

step 1

step 2

step 3

The Steps

Draw the Following Steps

step 4

step 5

step 6

The Steps

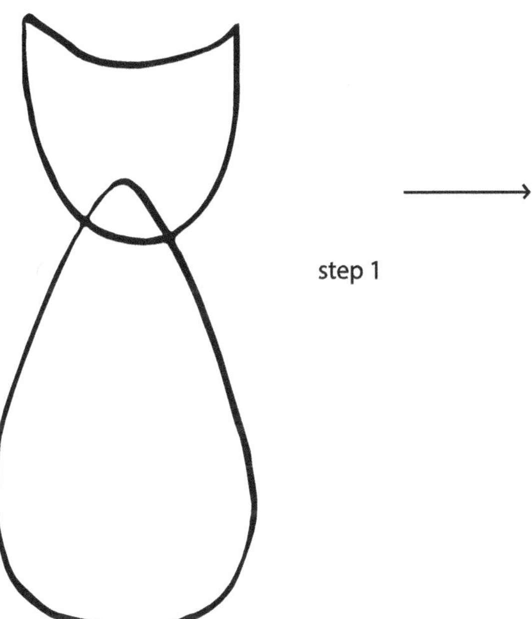

step 1

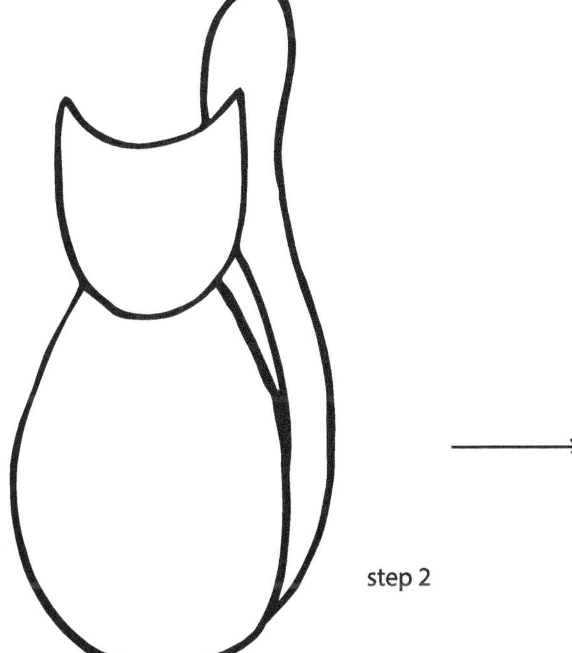

step 2

Draw the Following Steps

The Steps

step 3

step 4

Draw the Following Steps

The Steps

step 1

step 2

step 3

Draw the Following Steps

The Steps

step 4

step 5

38

The Steps

step 6

Draw the Following Steps

step 7

The Steps

Draw the Following Steps

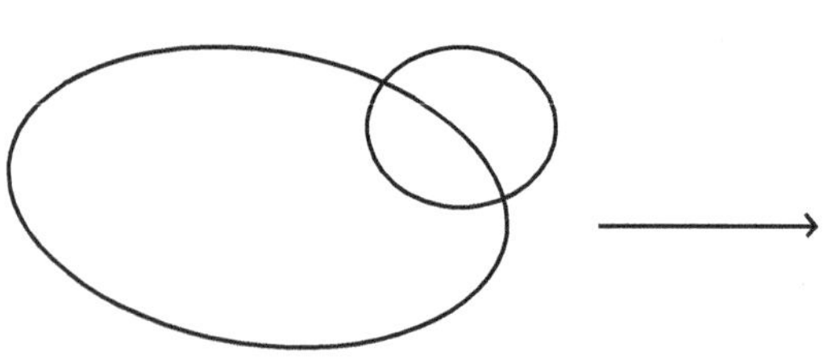

step 1

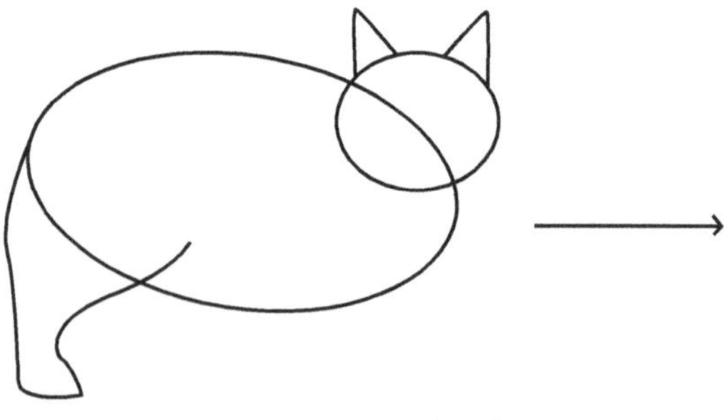

step 2

step 3

The Steps

step 4

step 5

step 6

Draw the Following Steps

DRAWING TUTORIAL EYES

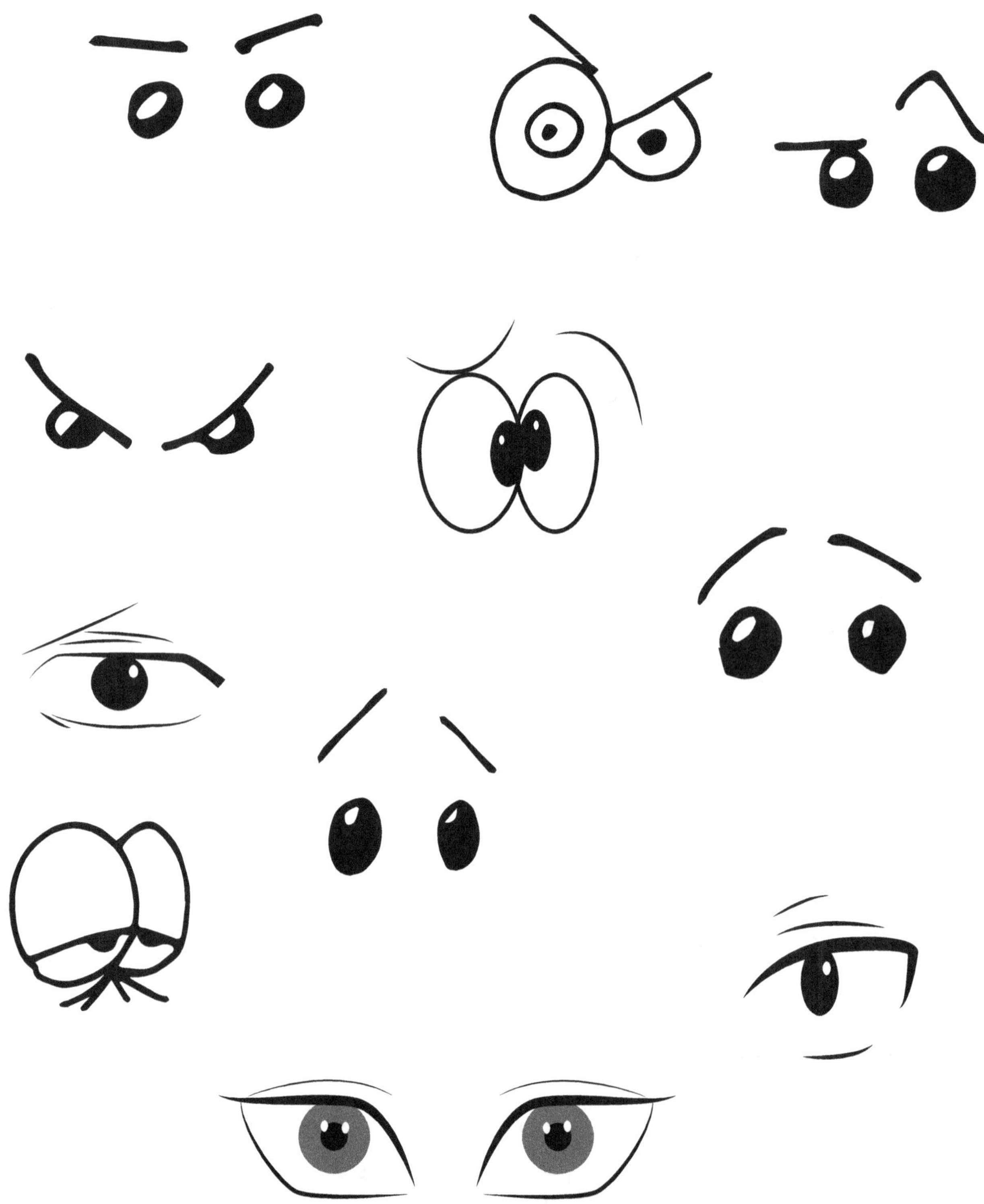

The Steps

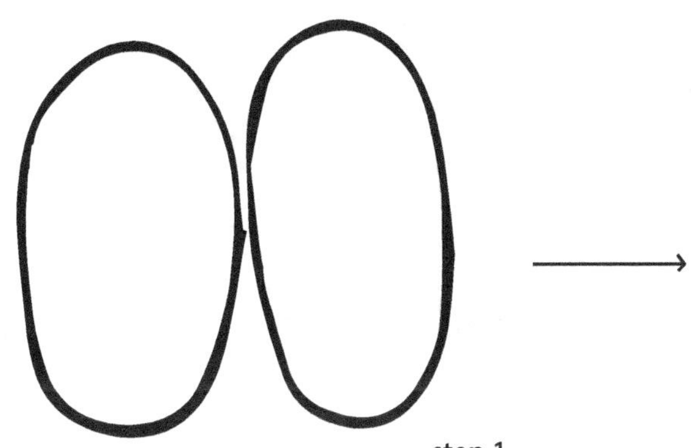

step 1

step 2

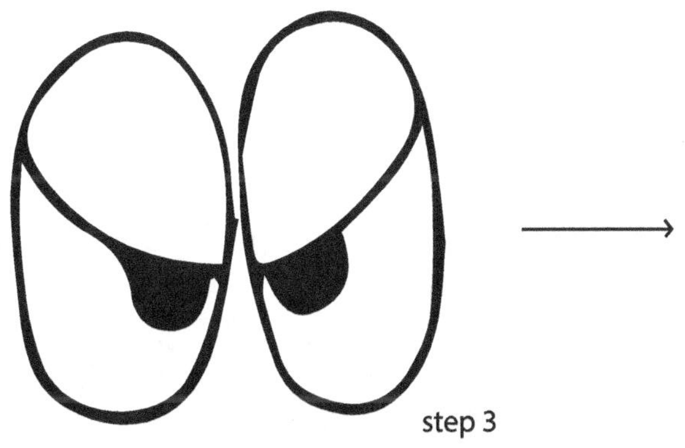

step 3

Draw the Following Steps

The Steps

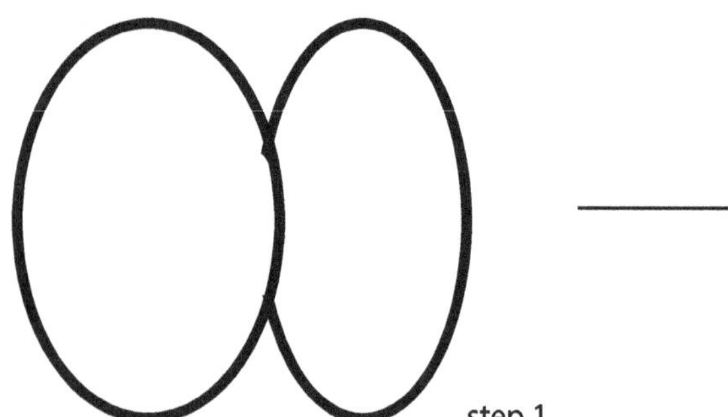

step 1

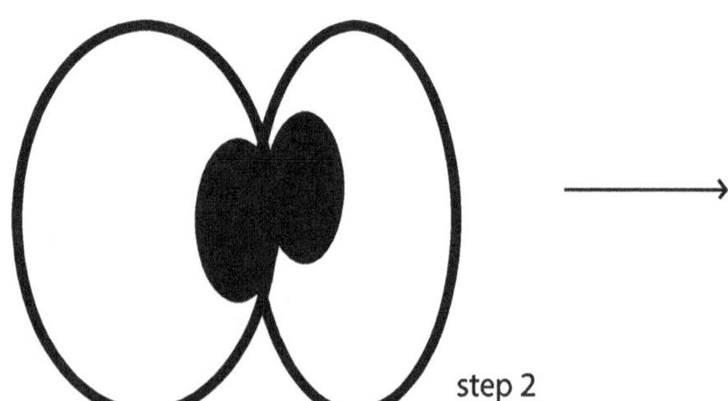

step 2

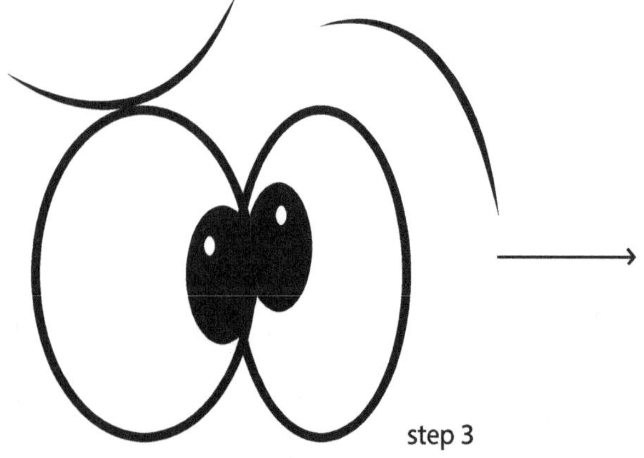

step 3

Draw the Following Steps

The Steps

Draw the Following Steps

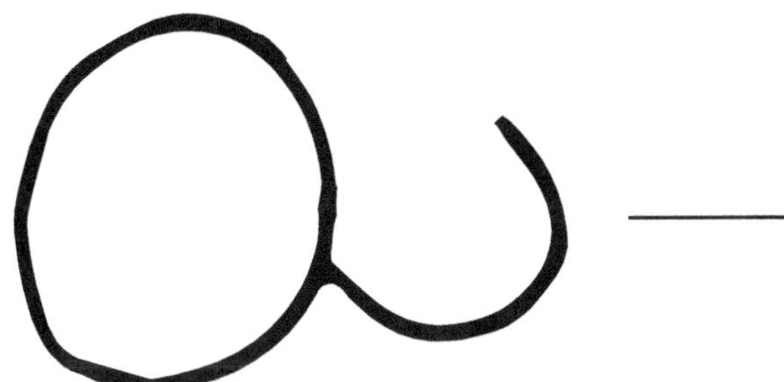

step 1

step 2

step 3

The Steps

Draw the Following Steps

step 1

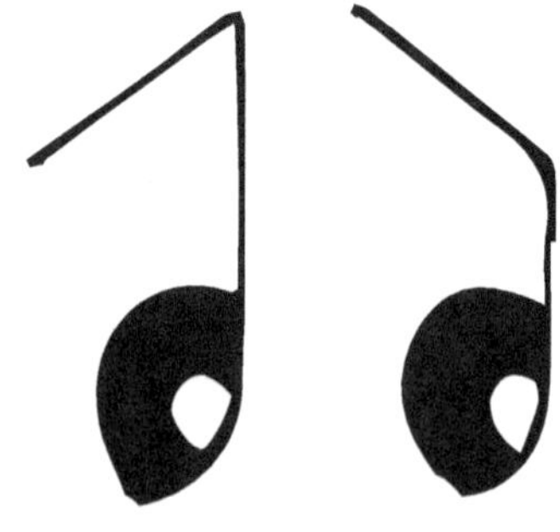

step 2

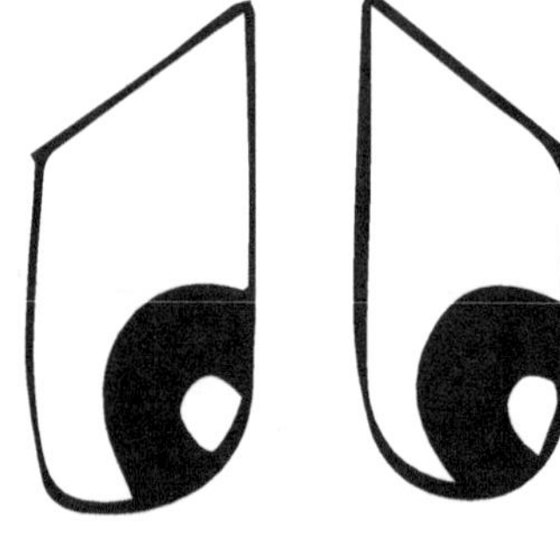

step 3

The Steps

step 1

step 2

step 3

The Steps

step 1

step 2

step 3

The Steps

step 1

step 2

step 3

The Steps

Draw the Following Steps

step 1

step 2

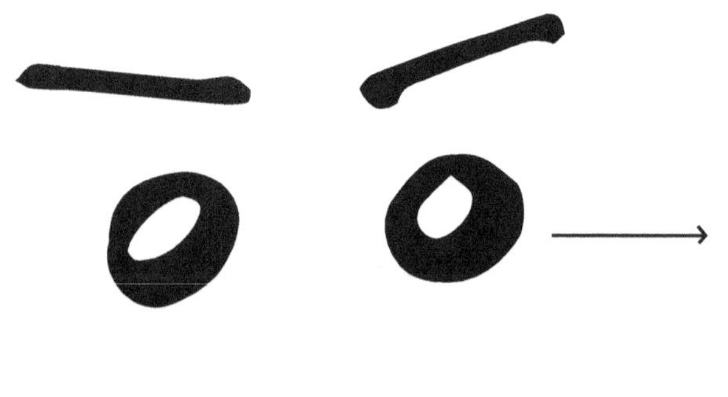

step 3

The Steps

step 1

step 2

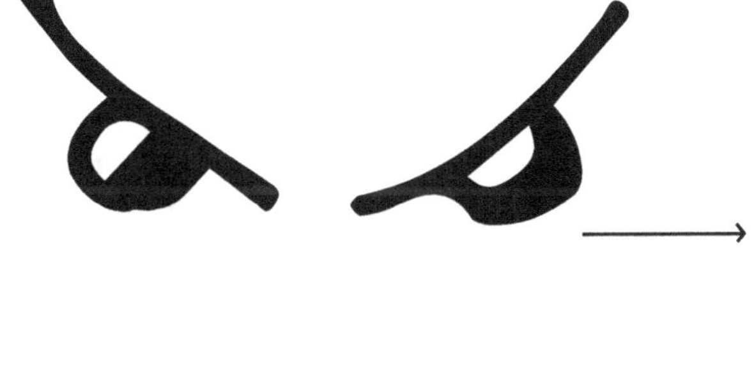

step 3

The Steps

Draw the Following Steps

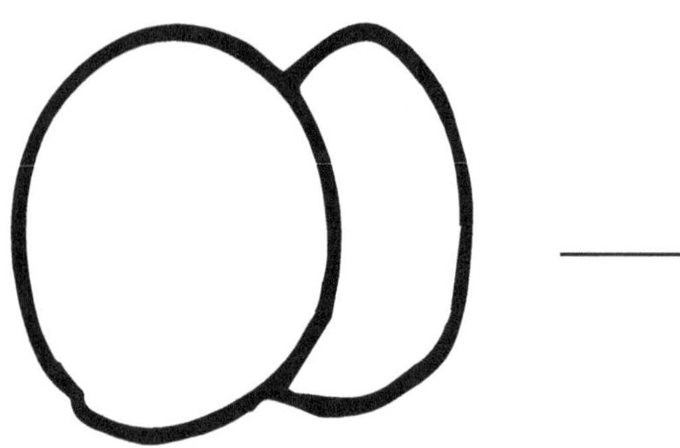

step 1

step 2

step 3

The Steps

Draw the Following Steps

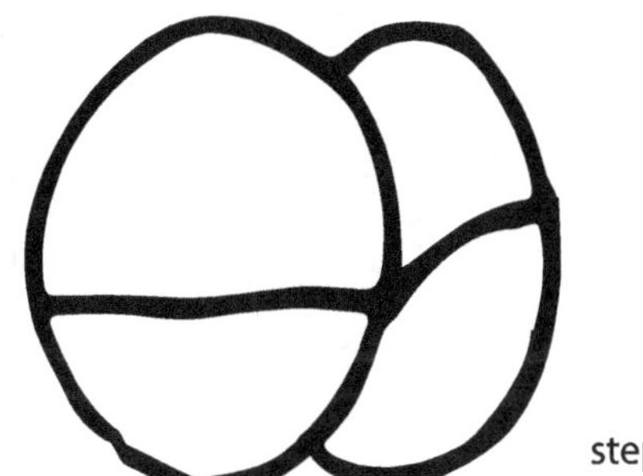

step 1

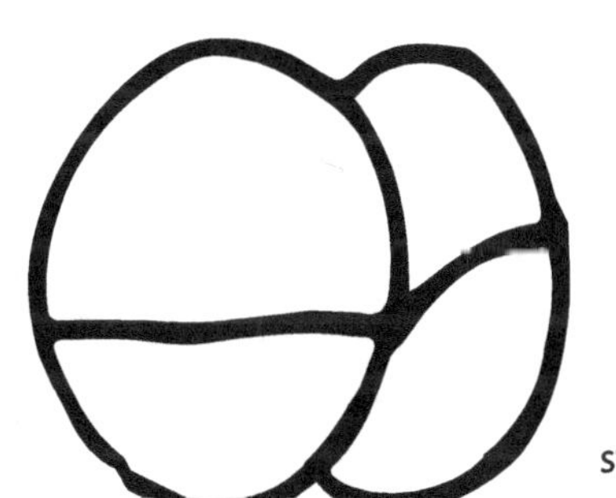

step 2

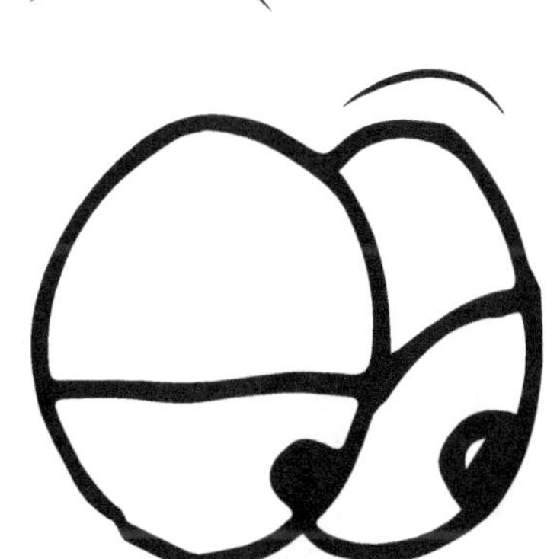

step 3

The Steps

Draw the Following Steps

step 1

step 2

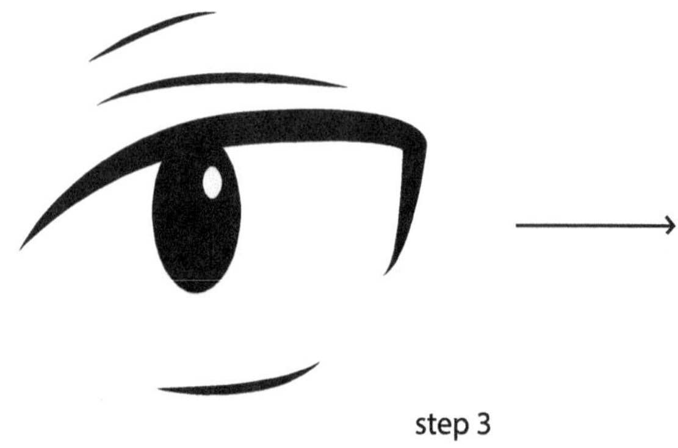

step 3

The Steps

step 1

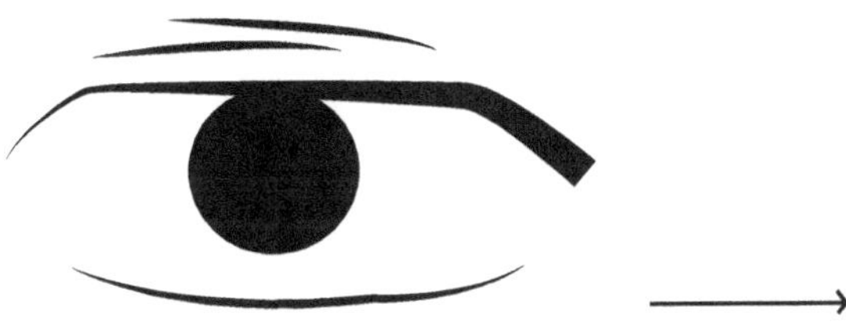

step 2

step 3

The Steps

Draw the Following Steps

step 1

step 2

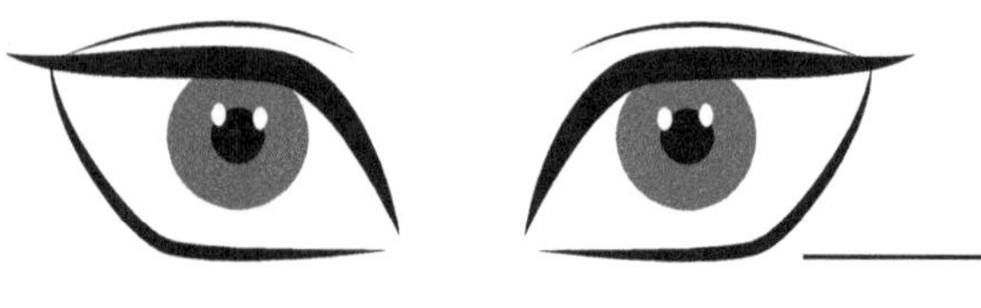

step 3

DRAWING TUTORIAL CARS

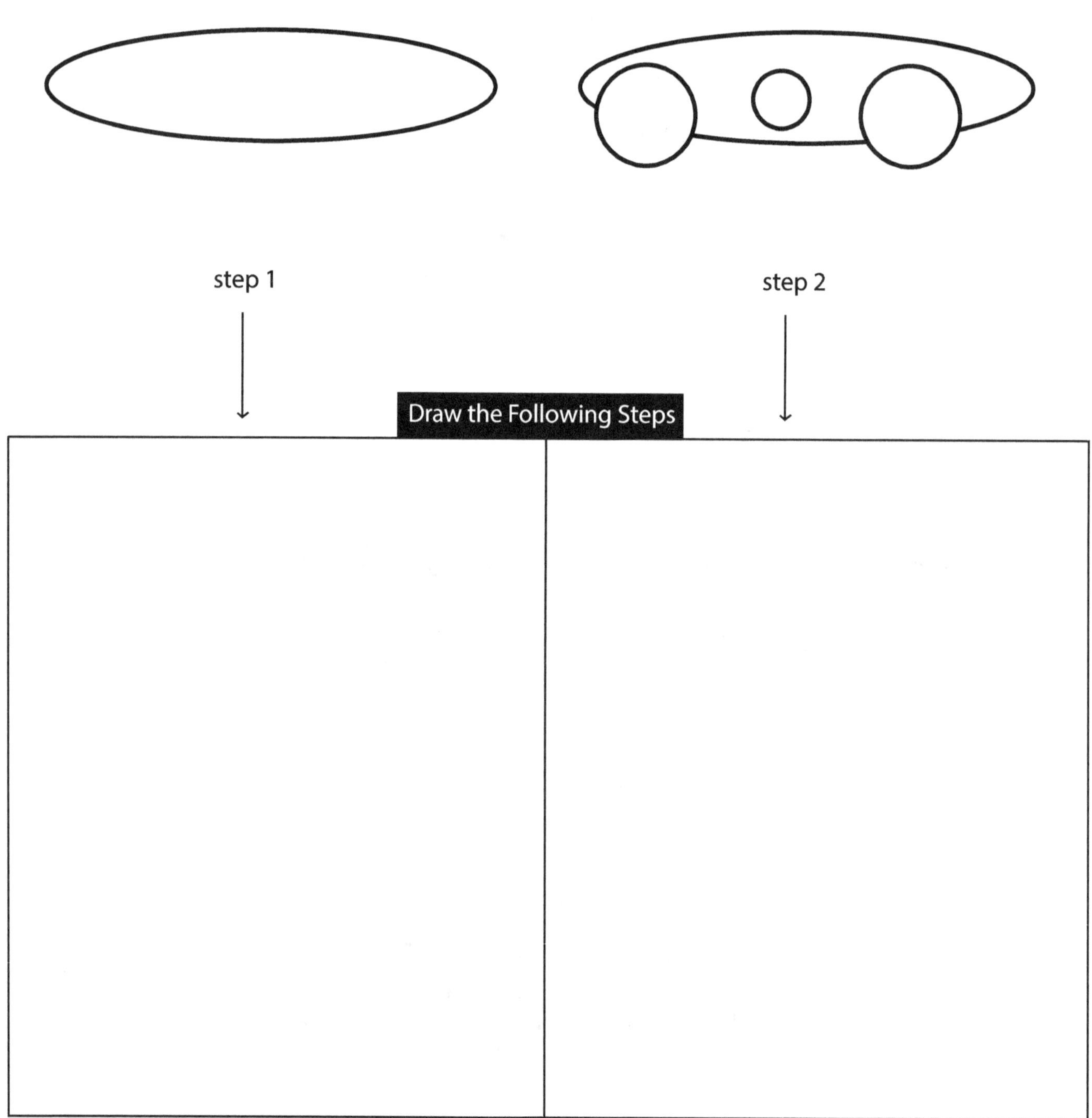
step 1
step 2
Draw the Following Steps

The Steps

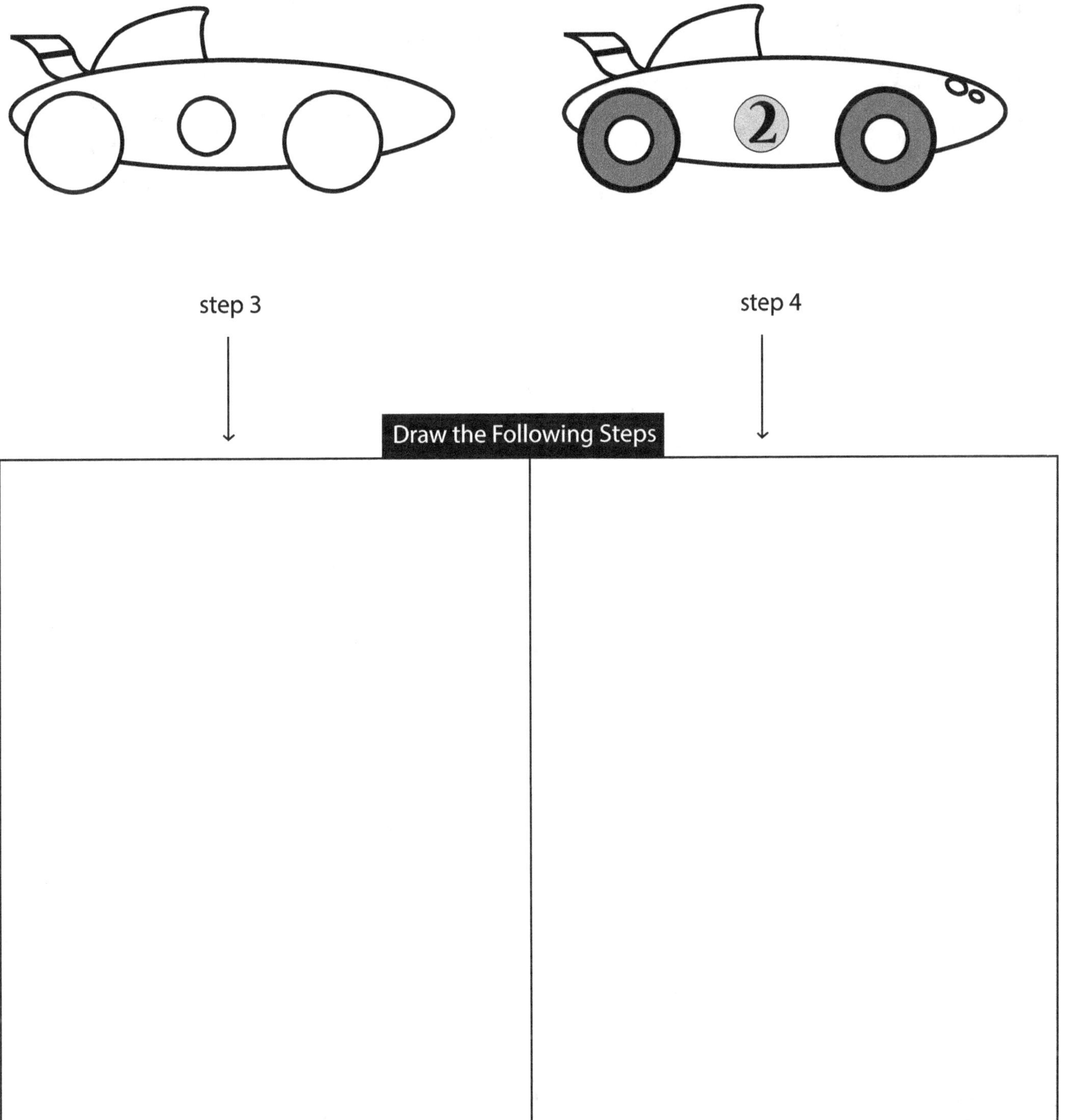

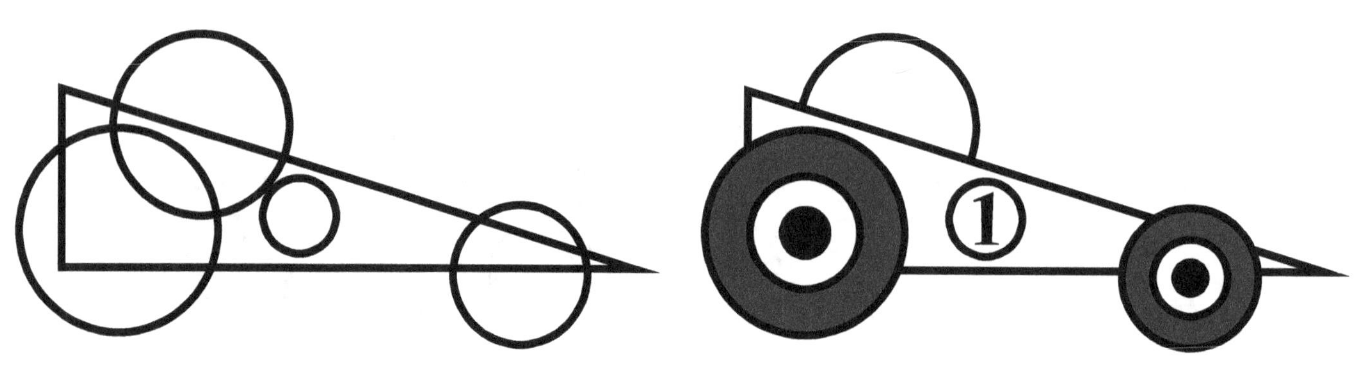

step 1

step 2

Draw the Following Steps

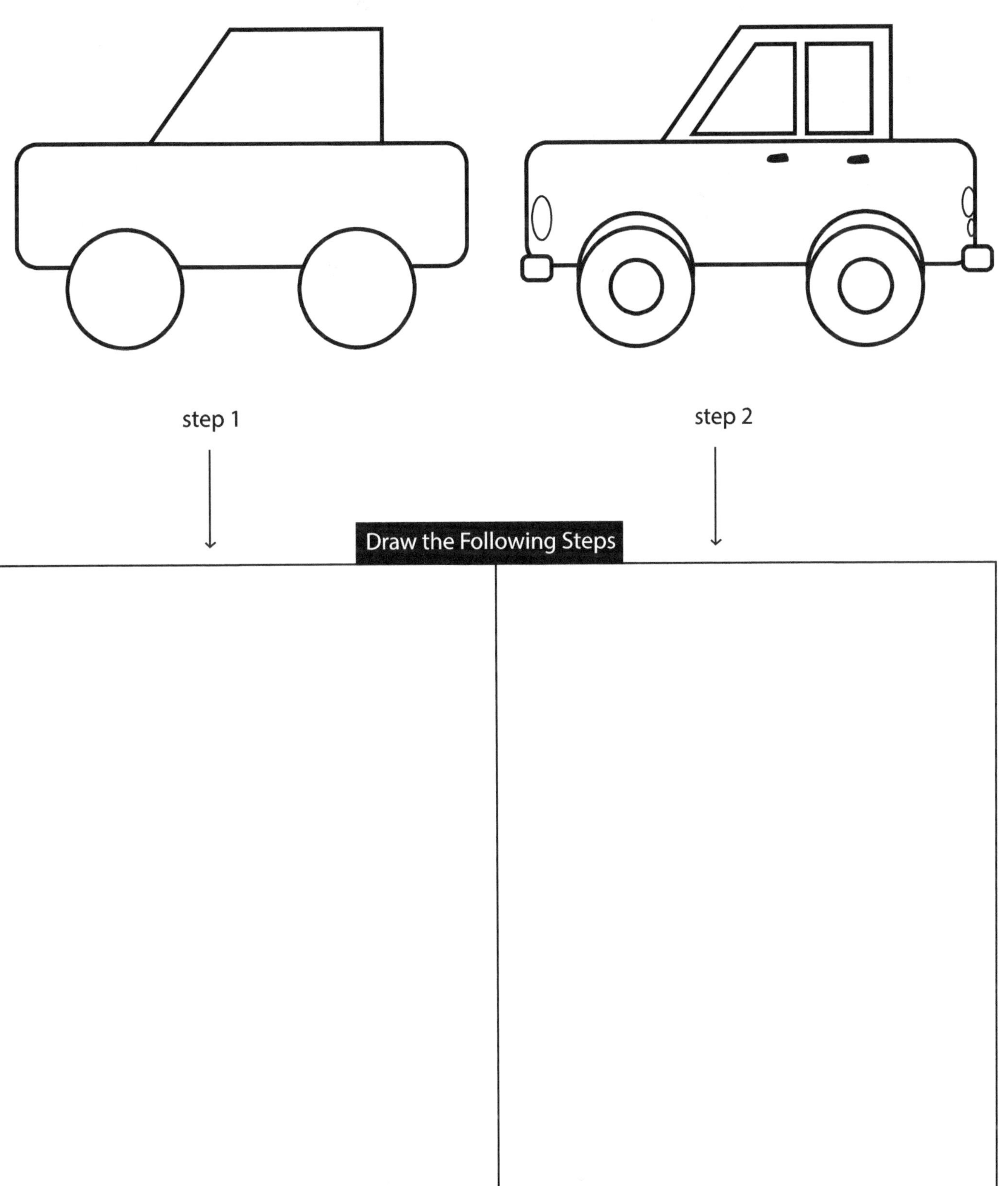
The Steps
step 1
step 2
Draw the Following Steps

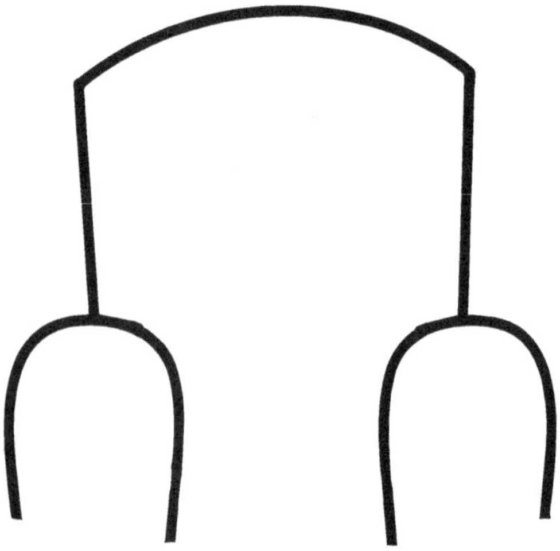

step 1

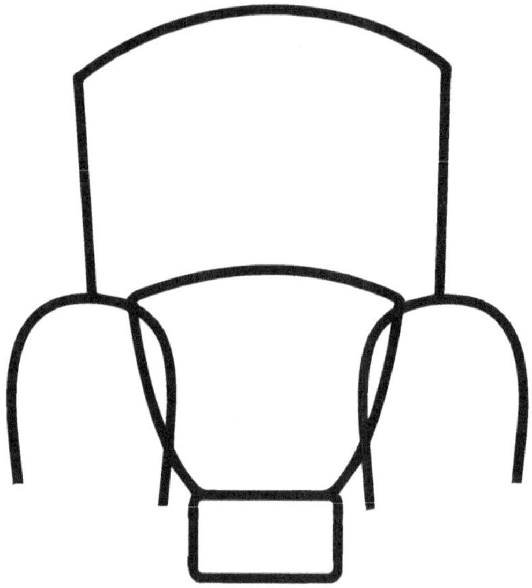

step 2

Draw the Following Steps

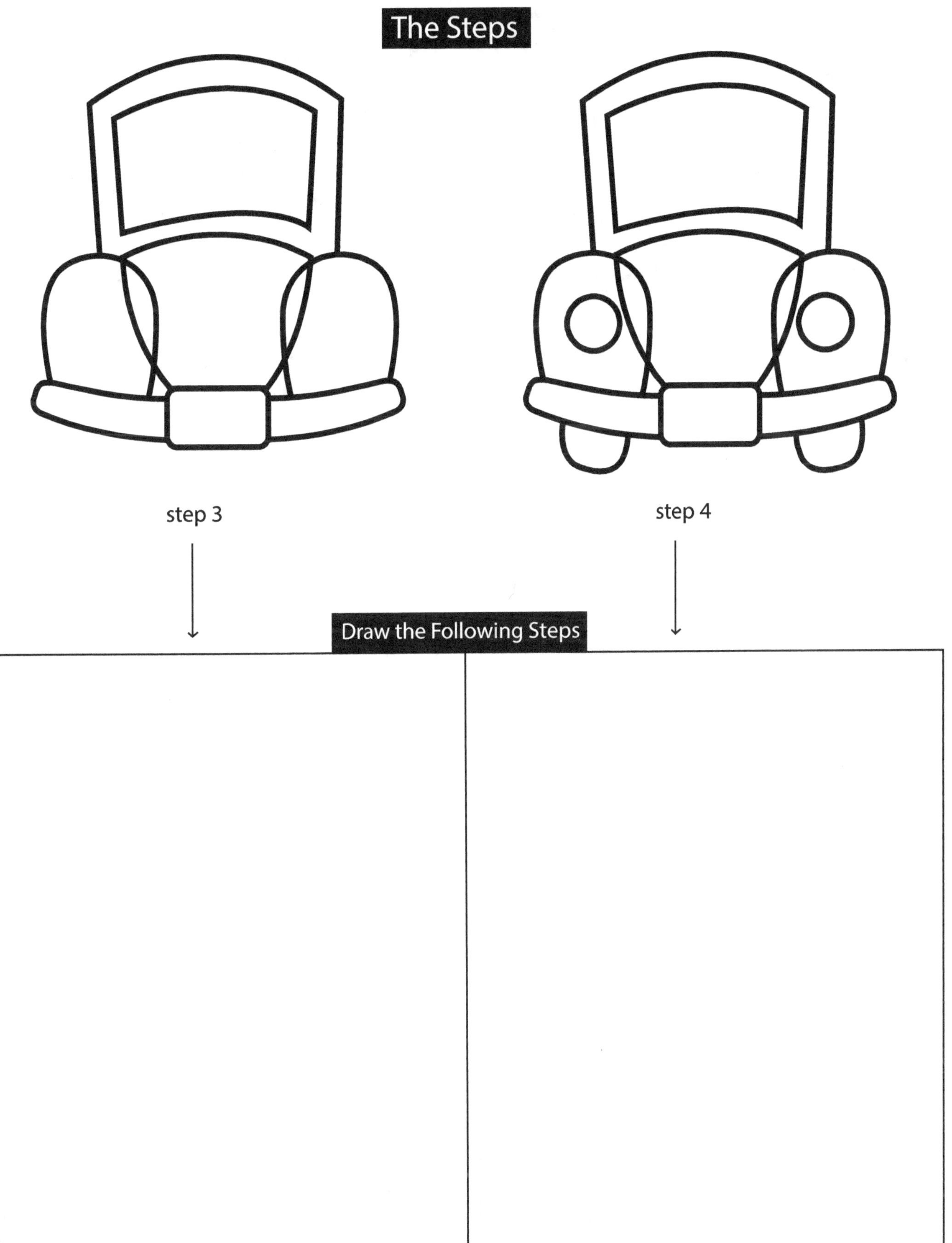
step 3
step 4
Draw the Following Steps

The Steps

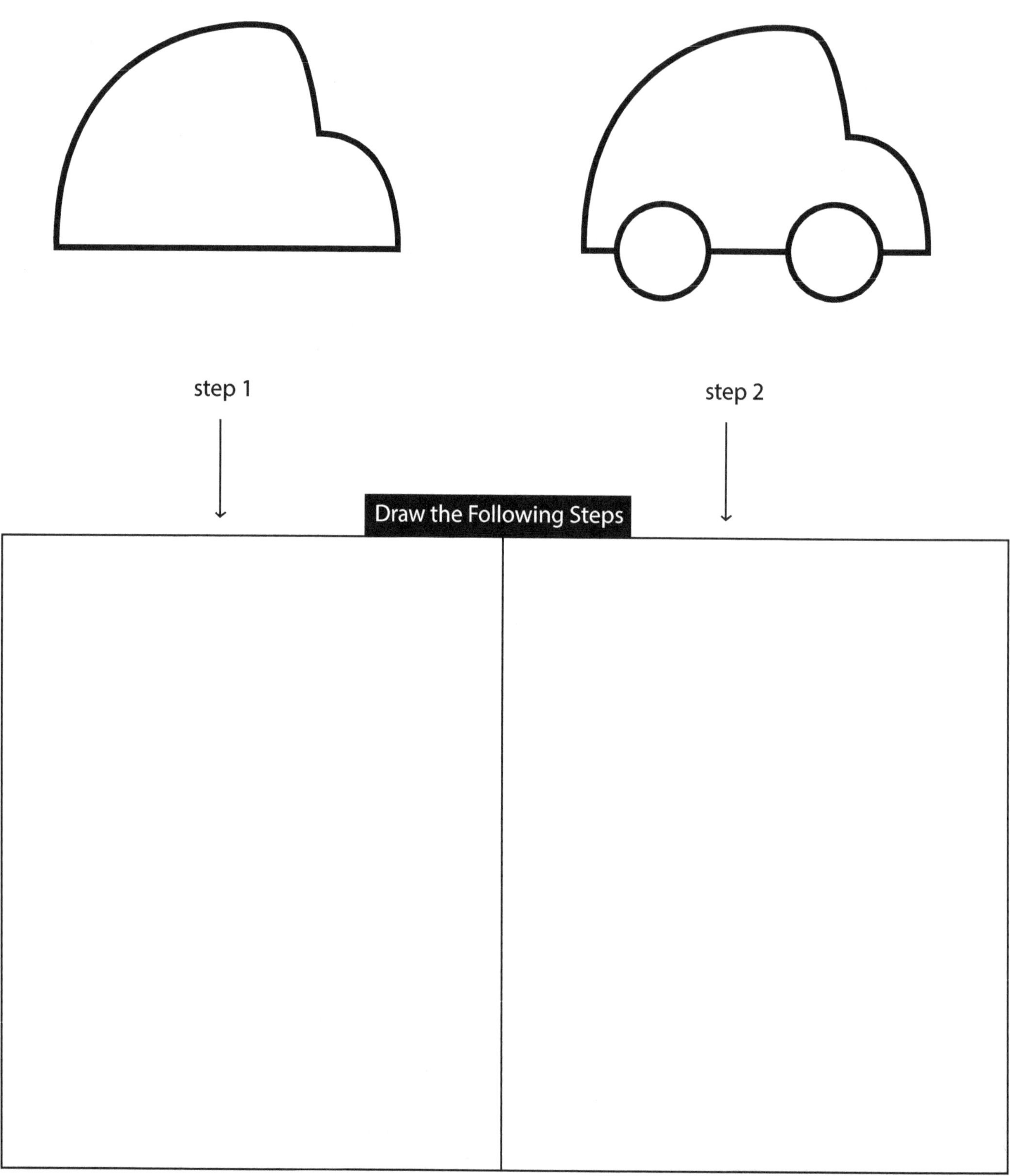

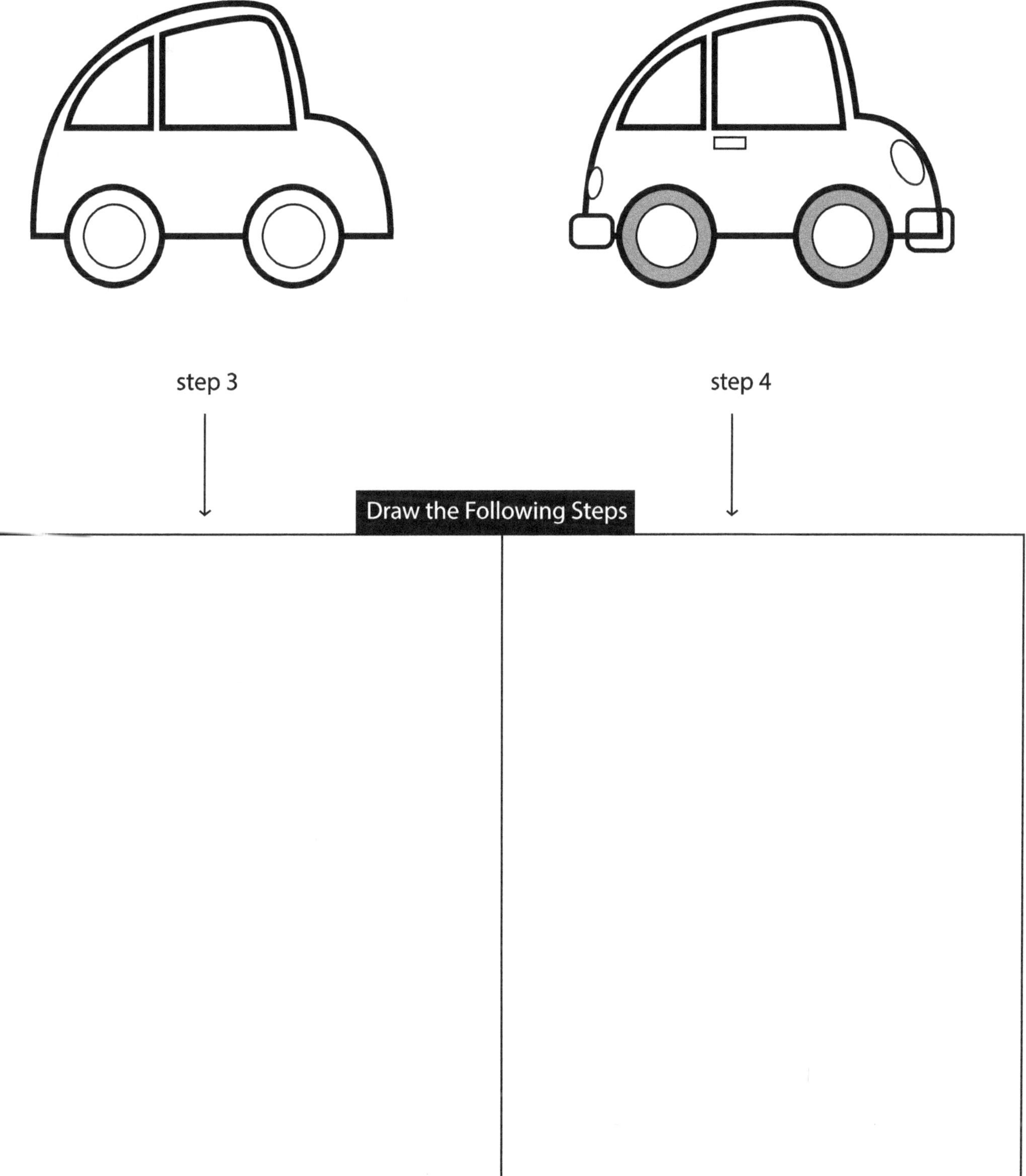

step 3
step 4
Draw the Following Steps